Cast Iron Cuisine
from Breakfast to D

Grandma's Skillet Reborn

by

Matt and Linda Morehouse

Published by
Paradise Cay Publications, Inc.
Arcata, CA

Cover design by Rob Johnson, www.johnsondesign.org
Book design and editing by Linda Morehouse, www.webuildbooks.com
Illustrations by Linda Morehouse

Contact Matt at matt@crowandbear.com or contact Linda at linda@webuildbooks.com

Printed in the United States of America
First Edition, Second Printing
ISBN 978-939837-84-6

Published by Paradise Cay Publications, Inc.
P. O. Box 29, Arcata, CA 95518-0029
800-736-4509, Fax 707-822-9163
paracay@humboldt1.com

To J. Buckminster Wadcutter III

who was there when we met on the beach

Contents

Introduction

First let us say what this book is *not* about. It is not a fast food book aimed at the soccer mom who needs to throw a meal on the table in half an hour (although a few recipes *do* serve that purpose). It is not a low-calorie, low-fat, "heart-healthy" cookbook (though efforts *have* been made to reduce fat, salt, and sugar content because that's just the smart thing to do). It is not an organic cookbook (though if you *want* to spend your money on organics it will not ruin any recipe).

This book *is* a compilation of hearty, time-tested, family-pleasing recipes that go well in a rustic environment but can still grace your formal city-home dining room. Most ingredients are commonly found at your local grocery store or in the fields, forest, and streams close by. A few more exotic ingredients, such as Sap Sago cheese or Mexican chocolate, etc., add such a distinctive flavor edge that they are worth acquiring from a specialty shop or from the online sources cited in Resources.

Most of the recipes in this book we have either created ourselves or significantly adapted from their traditional versions. The few that we have presented as we encountered them, we have attributed to their authors, where known.

This book is for the experienced family cook. We assume that you are familiar with the basic cooking methods; consequently, we do not explain in detail such processes as braising, sautéing, and the like. However, we do go into considerable detail discussing such processes as aging red meat and making stocks, which can provide that flavor edge that lifts a dish from the salubrious into the sublime.

Some of these recipes require four days from start to finish (thereby giving a new meaning to "slow food"); however, with the exception of making stock, no recipe requires more than one hour of total hands-on time.

All recipes that require long preparation times *can* be made more quickly, but there will be some significant loss of flavor. You *can* go to the supermarket, buy a cut of beef, and make, the very same day, a pot roast that will satisfy and nourish your family and guests. But it will not bear the inimitably dusky, intensely carnal flavor of the pot roast made from aged beef and homemade stock, the one we designate as Noble Pot Roast. You just have to taste this dish to believe it, and having tasted it, we guarantee the flavor will linger in your memory.

With the exception of the salads (which have been included for their flavor and texture contrast and because they're what we set on our own table), all these recipes can be made using cast iron cookware—indeed, the flavor of most dishes is enhanced thereby.

Cast iron cooking has been around since the 14ᵗʰ century, when cast iron was first smelted in China. New cast iron cookware is readily available, though we find it less user-friendly than the fine old pieces that have been seasoned through years and years of use and loving care.

There is a fine sufficiency—nay, a plethora--of antique and new ironware available on eBay at surprisingly reasonable prices. The best pieces come from the nineteenth century American foundries such as Griswold, Volrath, Wagner, etc., and can still be found at garage sales and flea markets. (See Cast Iron Care, following two pages.) They are worth seeking out, for you will soon become attached to your cast iron ware—especially your lidded skillet—and will consider it your best friend in the kitchen.

The recipes in this book are merely representative of what can be done in cast iron; this is by no means an exhaustive, encyclopedic work. It is an honest transcription of the meals that have nourished our families and guests for many years, occasionally garnering high praise and requests for recipes. When that happens now, we will simply hand them this cookbook.

—Matt and Linda Morehouse

Important Note: It's a wise strategy to read each recipe in its entirety at least twice before beginning the dish, to avoid surprises.

Choosing and Caring for Cast Iron Ware

Cast iron ware is our "go to" choice for just about all cooking in the kitchen as well as over the campfire. We have one Griswold #8 (affectionately called Grizzy Eight) with lid at home and one at the ranch. Of *all* our kitchen appliances, they are the most used.

Here are some of the dishes we like to cook in the Grizzy Eight: Chicken Marsala, Short Ribs of Beef, chunks of stew meat (beef, lamb, venison, goat, whatever), hash brown potatoes, Creekside, and Mountain Bread. We always bake our pies, even our cookies, in cast iron.

A cast iron Dutch oven is especially good for pot roasts, for it will produce a moist and tender meal every time. (For pot roasts, we favor a 7-bone chuck, but just about any of the shoulder cuts will do. Avoid the more expensive cuts, as they don't have enough fat to make a good pot roast.) The pot roast can either be cooked on top of the stove or in the oven; in the oven is actually better, for the heat surrounds the Dutch oven.

Do get a Grizzy (or Dutch oven) with a lid. You want a nice tight seal on all top surfaces. A good lid will not only fit tightly on all top surfaces, but on its interior face will have some device for returning moisture to the pan: ridges or points on which the steam condenses and drips back into the pan, self-basting the meat. Don't buy a lid without this feature.

When seeking cast iron cookware, we suggest you look at flea markets, garage sales, and ebay: it will be well worth your time. When looking for used ironware, avoid the newer ones made in Taiwan or China. The OLD American pieces are the best, being more finely milled than anything being produced today—look for the OLD Lodge, the Wagner, and Griswold names.

Follow the instructions for the care of your modern cast iron ware, but here's how we treat our Grizzy Eights. When you have finished cooking and have removed the food, let the skillet cool, then wipe it out gently with hot soapy water, rinse it well, dry it well, and put it back on the shelf.

Another very effective way of cleaning it, especially if there are particles of food stuck to it, is to throw in about half a cup of plain old table salt and use it as an abrasive to scour it with a siderag. Worst case, if food really gets baked on, put it back on the stove with a little water, gently boil it while scraping with a spatula or wooden spoon. A wooden spatula works very well. If you're not going to use it for a long while, apply a light coating of mineral oil and put it away. We like mineral oil instead of vegetable oil or meat oils because it will not turn rancid over a period of time. If you're using it on a daily or weekly basis this isn't necessary.

As for restoring an old, dirty piece of cast iron you've been lucky enough to find at a flea market or yard sale, here is the advice of Gregory Stahl, founder of the Wagner and Griswold Society:

"There are many ways to resuscitate cast iron that has seen years of abuse. If you are going to clean just a couple of pieces of iron, spray them with EZ OFF oven cleaner, place them in a plastic bag, and seal the bag. Take the item out of the bag after a few days and most of the carbonized material will be easy to remove by scrubbing with hot water and soap. Other ways to clean involve soaking in a lye bath, using electrolysis, or submitting the ware to the cleaning cycle of your self-cleaning oven. Never sandblast cast iron cookware. Avoid the use of open fires to burn off the old material, as these methods can damage your cookware.

"Once you have the old crud off your cast iron cookware, you'll need to re-season it. There are many ways to season your cast iron. Simply warm your item to 400 degrees in the oven. Remove it and then when it is safe enough to handle, apply a very thin coat of shortening (e.g., Crisco, bacon grease, or the like) and remove all excess. Place the item back in the oven at 375 degrees for one hour and then turn off the oven and let it cool in the oven without opening the door.

"You can also use spray-on shortening, such as PAM. Be sure to only apply a thin coat and then wipe off anything you use to season, otherwise the item will be sticky and blotchy. If you make a mistake, just strip the item again and start over.

"For specific tips, instructions, and a pictorial of how to clean and season your pans, visit the Wagner and Griswold Society website at www.wag-society.org. These friendly members have a forum where you can ask questions and identify your cast iron cookware for free. You might even consider becoming a member of this group to receive their newsletter and participate in their annual conventions."

Cast iron ware likes to be used frequently; that's what maintains its seasoning and gives it a special patina. In a well seasoned skillet you should be able to fry an egg with a minimal amount of butter or oil. It should be able to perform as well as any of the modern nonstick pans.

A lot of people say you should not cook acid-based foods—such as tomatoes, lemons, etc.—in cast iron. This is very true if you are cooking in cast iron that has not been properly seasoned, for then your food may pick up a rusty iron flavor. However, once cast iron has been properly seasoned, this is not a problem.

This book assumes that you are operating in a normal, well-equipped family kitchen, both at home and wherever else you may roam. In addition to that basic equipment, here are some tools and appliances that we have found especially useful.

Hardware

We are fond of baking and roasting in cast iron skillets because of their superior heat transmission and nonstick qualities (when well seasoned). Our indispensable ironware collection includes these items :

cast iron skillets #3, #5, #8, #10, #12
lid for #8 skillet
cast iron Dutch oven with lid
cast iron bacon press
cast iron griddle (if your stove doesn't have one)
cast iron muffin tin
cast iron loaf pans
cast iron corn-stick pan

We also depend upon the following:

chinois
Sometimes called a "China cap." This is a *very* fine mesh strainer. It's also very expensive. But it's indispensable for making silky-smooth stocks and sauces.

coffee grinder
Also very useful for grinding spices and for reducing nuts to a flour for baking.

digital kitchen scale
Ours is a Salter, cost about $40, but there are many other good ones out there. Matt uses this when ingredients have to be measured exactly. The digital scale comes in handy when you buy a large portion of meat or fish and want to divide it into equal serving-size portions for subsequent vacuum sealing and freezing. For two of us, Matt figures 1 pound of fish and about ¾ pound of boneless meat for each serving.

digital timers

Polder is a good brand.

instant-read thermometer

Indispensable for making bread, chicken, meats—anything whose temperature is critical. Professional chefs will wear one in the top pocket of their jackets. They use it as often as their side rags . . . and so do the health inspectors.

Kitchen-Aid mixer

An all-around useful kitchen appliance. It comes with basic attachments; if you want, you can add the meat grinder and sausage stuffer. Matt uses this for making **City Bread**, grinding venison, whipping potatoes, stuffing sausage, and a lot of other purposes.

large coarse strainer, 6–8 inches in diameter

Matt uses this so much he usually has to retrieve it from the dishwasher before Linda gets a chance to run it through. It replaces a colander in most applications, saving pasta water and bean water for use in stocks and soups. Spend $10 or $12 and buy a good one at a restaurant supply store.

large fine strainer, 6–8 inches in diameter

We buy these at a restaurant supply store. We pay a little more for them, but they're worth it.

lazy susan

We keep a large (18-inch) one beside the stove. It holds all our cooking essentials (*mise en place*).

mandoline

We've never owned one, but have cast covetous eyes on them many times. They slice and dice, they julienne, they slice vegetables paper-thin. It's sort of like a vacuum sealer: we don't want to buy a cheap one, and the really good ones cost about $200.

mortar and pestle

This ancient implement brings thoughts of alchemy, wizards, retorts and such. Matt has a large and beautiful mortar and pestle made by Coors, the beer people. Though he uses the coffee grinder for small quantities of herbs and spices, he still brings down the mortar and pestle when he has a lot of herbs to grind. He likes the feel of it.

parchment paper

Essential for producing **Mountain Bread**.

remote thermometer/timer with meat probe

A most useful implement that allows you to measure the temperature of whatever's in the oven without opening the oven. It also has an alarm you can set to go off at the desired temperature.

side rags (white terry-cloth towels one foot square)

We always keep about half a dozen side rags beside our *mise en place*. An experienced cook or chef always uses a side rag rather than a potholder or mitten.

spray bottle

Useful for spritzing water into the oven when making bread. Also, put on fine-squirt, it keeps the dog out of the kitchen.

stockpots with spigots

If you really enjoy stockmaking, as some people do, these are a worthy investment. They're expensive and hard to find, but see Resources for a good lead on where to purchase one online.

ulu

Well known in Alaska as a chopping and flensing tool. We like its ease of handling for small chopping tasks. See page 148 for an illustration.

vacuum sealer

This is one of the most useful kitchen appliances we own. After wearing out two or three of the El-Cheapo's, we finally broke down and bought a $300 top-of-the-line unit from Cabelas. It's especially useful for processing food for freezing, and thus provides a good way to save and preserve leftovers. Ours occupies prime real-estate on our limited counter space. There are plenty of cheap ones out there, but don't be tempted. Get a good one. It'll outlast several less expensive models.

wooden spoons

These don't scratch your pans. They're also quiet and have a nice feel to them.

If you don't have all of the above, don't let that stop you from proceeding to cook from this book. Substitute whatever's available and keep your eyes open for the real thing.

Staples in the Larder

extra-virgin olive oil
What can we say? Matt's half Italian.

balsamic vinegar
The better it is, the more it costs.

dried wild mushrooms
Dried porcini and dried chanterelles can lift an ordinary dish into a gourmet experience. We find that the flavor of chanterelles has a special affinity for the dusky, gamey edge to goat meat.

sun-dried tomatoes
The moister and more succulent, the better.

crystallized candied ginger
We like Trader Joe's Organic Ginger Chunks. They come in small die-shaped cubes. Dense and chewy, their consistency reminds us of high-quality gumdrops.

dried sliced mangoes and other dried fruits
Good for snacking, but especially good for baking.

slivered almonds
We keep several different varieties of nuts on hand, but this is the one we turn to most often. Useful toasted, chopped, or just as is.

Mexican chocolate
Three familiar brand names are Casero, Ibarra, or Abuelita by Nestles. Used to make hot chocolate, this product comes in a six-sided paper cylinder containing six chocolate tablets, each scored into six pie-shaped pieces. A good quality brand consists of sugar, cocoa liquor, soy lecithin and cinnamon. Use as you would baker's chocolate, but be aware that it is sweeter, grainier, and has a slight cinnamon edge to its flavor.

sweetened condensed milk
Handy for making key lime pie surrogates. Also can be boiled in the can to make a caramel sauce.

nonfat dry milk powder
Useful for adding richness to baked products without requiring more flour to offset the liquid content of regular milk. When reconstituted, handy as a fresh milk substitute in recipes calling for milk.

turbinado sugar
We don't even keep refined white sugar in the house,

preferring this more nutritious, more flavorful, minimally processed sugar.

molasses

See previous entry.

blue agave nectar

An excellent low-glycemic liquid sweetener, useful for beverages, baking, or general household sweetening purposes. Extracted from the blue agave cactus, which should be familiar to you tequila aficionados.

sea salt

More nutritious and more flavorful than ordinary table salt. We prefer Redmond RealSalt, mined from ancient sea beds sealed during the Jurassic era, thus free of all modern pollutants. This slightly pink salt contains more than 50 trace minerals, including iodine.

Neufchatel cheese

Lower in calories than cream cheese, but just as useful.

Parmesan cheese in all its forms

See comment under extra-virgin olive oil.

Sap Sago cheese

This hard grating cheese from Switzerland lasts until you use it up. Sap Sago has a pungent, smoky flavor that adds zest to spaghetti. Some consider it an acquired taste, so test a little before using lavishly. We dote on it.

Thai peanut satay sauce

Tiny dabs of it make a wonderful, unexpected dressing for a fruit salad.

hoisin sauce

This has rescued many an experimental fish or chicken dish that fell flat. (Hey, nothing ventured, nothing gained. But relax; every recipe in this book has passed our critical taste tests.)

mango chutney

Especially welcome as a condiment for ordinary hamburgers. Our guests have been known to go through a whole jar at one sitting.

guajillo chiles

Mild red chiles available in the Mexican section of most supermarkets. Useful for adding depth and flavor to stews, soups, and chilis.

nopalitos
Slivers of cactus (nopal) with a distinctive tangy (not spicy) flavor. Think of it as "matchsticks" of pickled cactus. Available in any supermarket with a decent Mexican foods section.

kombu
A gray or dark brown sea vegetable popular in Japanese cooking. High in potassium, iodine, calcium, and vitamins A and C, kombu adds a distinctive flavor to stocks. It's available in well-stocked health foods sections of large supermarkets, or see Resources.

natural black walnut flavor
Long a favorite of fine confectioners, this can be hard to find, but its inimitable flavor makes it worth the search. We found some at Butte Creek Mills, an old-fashioned, water-powered, stone-ground flour mill in Eagle Point, Oregon.

Marigold bouillon powder
A useful low-salt vegetable bouillon. See Resources.

Bragg's liquid amino seasoning
A very healthful flavoring agent.

Mise en Place
(Necessaries at the cooking station)

Matt keeps these on a large lazy susan close to the stove:

canola oil
extra-virgin olive oil
dry red wine
dry white wine
white and balsamic vinegars
vermouth
Marsala and sherry wines
nonstick cooking spray
salt and pepper
shaker of white flour

These he keeps close by, in a cabinet:

sun-dried tomatoes
dried wild mushrooms
whole peppercorns

Many of these recipes work quite well for lunch--or even dinner. Who says eggs are only for breakfast? (For that matter, who says breakfast must contain eggs?)

Up at the ranch, we never know who might wander in, so we like dishes that can stretch. Our old favorites, **Creekside** and **Joe's Special**, are quite expandable.

And unexpected chores can call a person away just as the meal's ready to be served. If the bear's gonna bite through the water line, he doesn't ask if it's convenient for the residents of the Crow 'n Bear.

So we doubly appreciate the dish that can wait patiently on the wood stove or in the oven's warming drawer. **Ham and Red-Eye Gravy** is particularly good at that kind of thing.

And speaking of getting called away unexpectedly, it's nice to have something to tuck in your pocket for the hike up to the spring. **Apple Fingers, Maple Puffs, Skillet Mango Muffin, Skillet Strawberry Muffin,** and **Strawberry Macadamia Scones** all fill the bill.

Now, we're a gustatorily open-minded pair. Ingredients such as oysters or lamb kidneys bring us delight, rather than cause us suspicion. So you'll find here the traditional **Hangtown Fry**, as well as the British breakfast favorite, **Lamb Kidneys and Broiled Tomatoes.**

At first reading, you may be skeptical of some of these recipes, such as **Hummelgum** or **Breakfast Lasagna.** (In the lunch section, **Peanut Butter, Bacon, and Dill Pickle Sandwich** comes to mind.) But try them before you pass judgment. That nobbly pebble in the path just might be a gold nugget.

Apple Fingers

This recipe makes two large apple turnovers, each of which cuts into six to eight finger-sized servings good for breakfast, dessert, or snacks.

Crust
3 cups unbleached flour
¾ teaspoon sea salt
½ cup olive oil
4 tablespoons butter, divided

Filling
2 tablespoons pecans, finely chopped
2 tablespoons raisins
1 crisp apple (Fuji, Gala, or similar)
2 tablespoons brown sugar
½ teaspoon cinnamon
¼ teaspoon nutmeg
1 tablespoon flour
½ teaspoon lime juice
2 tablespoons molasses
12 cloves

In a large mixing bowl, sift flour with salt, then drizzle in the olive oil, stirring with a fork. Cut in 2 tablespoons of the butter, setting the rest aside for the filling. Add 10 tablespoons ice water, stirring well. Form into two balls. Between two pieces of waxed paper, roll each ball into a 10" diameter circle and set aside.

To make filling, combine pecans and raisins. Cut apple into quarters, core the quarters, then slice each quarter lengthwise as fine as you can. Cut each set of sliced quarters crosswise, slicing as fine as you can. Sift brown sugar with cinnamon, nutmeg, and flour.

Onto one rolled-out ball of crust, place half of the fine apple slices, keeping to one side of the circle. Add half the pecans and raisins mixture. Sprinkle half the sugar/flour/spice mixture over the apples, pecans, and raisins. Sprinkle half the lime juice evenly over the nut and fruit mix, drizzle one tablespoon of molasses evenly over all, and dot with one tablespoon butter, cut fine.

Lifting one side of the waxed paper, fold the uncovered half of the crust over the covered half. Peel paper away. Fold edges of the packet back on themselves, then crimp with a fork. Poke six cloves into the top of the crust at even intervals.

Using two spatulas, lift filled packet from the waxed paper and place it to one side in an ungreased #12 (14-inch) cast iron skillet, leaving room for the other packet beside it. Repeat process with remaining ingredients.

Bake in preheated 425 degree oven for 30 minutes or until crust is browned and packets are sizzling. Remove from oven and let cool completely. Cut into slices the width of two fingers each.

Makes 12 to 16 servings.

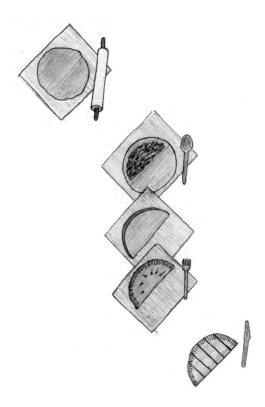

Hummelgum

As a child, Aunt Ruth would not eat eggs. In order to coax some down her, her father invented this dish. It looks awful, but it tastes mighty good. This recipe has been tried on three generations of children since then. In fact, it's become such a family favorite that Christmas morning is not the same without Hummelgum.

1 pound bacon
5 large shredded wheat pillows
6 eggs
2 tablespoons butter

In a large cast iron skillet, fry the bacon to stage of your taste. Remove from skillet, drain on paper towels, chop into medium dice. Pour most of the fat out of the skillet, leaving about a tablespoon. Put chopped bacon back in skillet over medium heat.

Crumble shredded wheat over bacon. Crack eggs over the mixture. Stir with a spatula, breaking eggs and mixing well. When eggs begin to set, add butter; stir to melt.

Serve immediately over warm dishes. Hummelgum does not hold well. Serves 6.

Variations:

Drizzle some of the remaining bacon fat over before serving, OR completely eliminate bacon fat and use a little extra butter, OR completely eliminate butter and bacon fat and use olive oil instead.

However, any way you cut it, this is not a low-calorie, low-cholesterol dish, so you might just as well slather on the grease and enjoy.

Breakfast Lasagna

Contributed by Lisa Morehouse, who ate some at a potluck breakfast event and was so impressed she worked it out at home. Lisa says you can substitute any meat for the bacon.

15 slices soft white bread
3 cups shredded Cheddar cheese
1 pound bacon
18 eggs
1½ cups milk
black pepper to taste

Grease a 13x9 pan. Cover bottom with 5 slices of bread. Distribute 1 cup shredded cheese evenly and generously on top of the layer of bread.

Cook bacon (here's where your cast iron comes in) and crumble finely. Sprinkle half of the crumbles evenly over the cheese.

Add a layer of bread, top it with another cup of cheese and more bacon crumbles.

Add a final layer of bread. Top with the last cup of cheese.

Into a large bowl crack eggs; beat together with milk. Add black pepper to taste.

Pour whipped egg/milk mixture over the whole thing, cover with plastic wrap and refrigerate overnight.

Next morning, preheat oven to 350, and bake uncovered 1 hour. Cut in squares and serve hot.

Serves 8 to 10.

Skillet Mango Muffin

2 eggs
⅓ cup olive oil
½ cup water
2 teaspoons lime juice
1½ cups unbleached flour
½ cup dried milk powder
⅓ cup turbinado sugar
1 tablespoon baking powder
1 teaspoon orange zest
½ cup preserved dried mango, cut in tiny slivers
½ cup slivered almonds

Beat eggs until fluffy. Add olive oil in a steady stream, continuing to beat mixture until it reaches the consistency of mayonnaise. Stir in water and lime juice; blend well and set aside.

In a separate bowl combine flour, dried milk powder, baking powder, sugar, and orange zest. Add dry ingredients to the wet ingredients a little at a time, stirring until well combined. Add mango slivers to batter; stir to mix well.

Distribute batter evenly in an ungreased but well-seasoned 6-inch cast iron skillet. Top with slivered almonds.

Bake at 375 degrees for 30 minutes or until top is lightly browned and a toothpick comes out clean. Remove from oven; set on a rack to cool. To serve, cut in pie-shaped wedges while still warm.

Serves 6.

Skillet Strawberry Muffin

This tasty little breakfast for two uses no added sugar.

2 tablespoons butter
¼ cup slivered almonds
2 eggs
¼ cup dried strawberries, snipped
1 tablespoon orange zest
½ teaspoon cardamom (optional)
½ cup flour
2 teaspoons baking powder
2 tablespoons Neufchatel cheese

In a #3 cast iron skillet, melt butter. Swirl almonds in butter to coat. Set aside to cool.

Beat the eggs until light and fluffy. Strain cooled melted butter into eggs, reserving almonds. Add strawberries, orange zest, and cardamom (if using).

Mix flour and baking powder. Add to wet mixture and stir thoroughly.

Turn into the same skillet you melted the butter in. Dot batter with Neufchatel cheese. Top with buttered almonds.

Bake in preheated 375 degree oven for 15 minutes, or until a toothpick comes out clean.

Serve with extra Neufchatel cheese for spreading, if desired. Serves 2.

Sour Cream Pancakes

These light and delicate pancakes have a flavor reminiscent of buttermilk, but with a slightly sweeter edge.

2 eggs
1 tablespoon olive oil
1 teaspoon vanilla
3 tablespoons turbinado sugar
½ cup light sour cream
1 cup flour
1 teaspoon baking soda
¼ cup dried milk
½ teaspoon sea salt
½ cup water

Beat eggs until light and fluffy. Beat in olive oil, vanilla, and sugar and continue to beat until sugar is melted. Add sour cream; beat until mixture is well blended.

Sift flour with baking soda, dried milk, and salt. Add wet mixture to dry mixture, stirring in water until batter is desired consistency. If you like your pancakes thin, you may need to add a little extra water.

Spoon onto preheated cast iron griddle, turning once when bubbles form. Makes about 24 pancakes of 3-inch diameter.

Variation: Honey-Smoked Stacks

For each serving:
6 sour cream pancakes
1 tablespoon softened Neufchatel cheese
2 deli slices honey-smoked (or other) ham, warmed
3 tablespoons walnuts, chopped very fine.

Lightly spread cheese on 2 warm sour cream pancakes. Stack pancakes. On top of cheese-spread pancakes place 1 deli slice honey-smoked ham (warmed), then 1 tablespoon walnuts chopped very fine. Stack with another 2 cheesed pancakes, another slice of warmed deli ham, and more walnuts. Top stack with 2 pancakes and a final sprinkling of walnuts. Serve with warmed maple syrup. One full recipe of pancakes serves 4.

Joe's Special

This recipe was created at Original Joe's on Broadway in San Francisco many years ago. Although we did not create it, it so perfectly fits the tenor of this book that we felt we must include it. This makes a hearty breakfast, lunch, or dinner. A simple, complete meal in one skillet.

1 pound any lean ground red meat
1 tablespoon canola oil
1 package frozen spinach, chopped (or fresh spinach, chopped, if you have it)
2 medium onions, chopped
6 cloves garlic, crushed, peeled, and diced
½ pound fresh white mushrooms, sliced
4 eggs
salt and pepper to taste
Worcestershire to taste

In a large cast-iron skillet, brown the meat in oil. While the meat is browning, prepare the frozen spinach according to package directions and drain. If using fresh spinach, simply steam it until it wilts.

Remove browned meat from skillet and set aside. Pour off excess fat from the skillet. Throw in onions, garlic, and mushrooms and sauté until onions are translucent. Throw meat back in skillet.

Add drained spinach and mix well, stirring continually, over medium to low heat.

You are now in a holding pattern if you want to be. Cover, turn heat real low, and make sure everybody's ready to sit down.

Uncover, turn heat to high, and when everything starts to sizzle, crack and throw in the eggs. Turn and stir with spatula until eggs have just set. Sprinkle with salt, pepper, and Worcestershire to taste. Place skillet on table and let everybody dig in.

Serves 4 hungry adults.

Serve with ketchup, Worcestershire, Tabasco, and any other condiments that please your crowd. I have a friend who likes mustard on his.

For variations, see following page.

For **Italian Joe's**, substitute Italian sausage or any other type of sausage for the ground beef.

For **Mexican Joe's,** use chorizo.

You can also use any other chopped leafy green vegetables, such as bok choy, chard, mustard greens, collard greens, or any combination thereof.

Toasted **Mountain Bread** (page 130) goes very well.

Hangtown Fry

There is a town in California's gold country, on Route 49, that used to be called Hangtown but is now known as Placerville. Therein lies the genesis of this recipe (which is basically just a large omelet).

In the 1850s, so the legend goes, a miner who had been working the Shirttail Bend rode into town on his burro. Fresh from the digs, he came to town rich in gold and rich in appetite. He walked into the El Dorado Hotel and said, "I'm hungry. What's the most expensive stuff you got to eat?" And he slammed his poke down on the bar.

The bartender said, "The most expensive food we have here is oysters shipped from San Francisco, eggs shipped from Petaluma, and bacon from Sacramento. The eggs are a dollar a dozen; the oysters are two dollars a dozen; the bacon's a dollar a pound. What'll you have?"

The miner replied, "I'll have a pound of bacon, a dozen of your oysters, and a dozen of your eggs."

The bartender said, "And how would you like that?"

The miner answered, "Just throw 'em in a skillet and fry 'em all up."

The bartender relayed the order to the cook, and thereupon was born the now-famous Hangtown Fry. Think of it as an omelet with an attitude.

1 pound bacon
1 cup bread crumbs
1 dozen medium oysters, shucked
1 dozen eggs

Fry the bacon in your largest cast-iron skillet, for this is surely what was used for the original recipe. Don't overcook it: It should be limp, not crisp.

Remove the bacon, and pour off most of the fat. Dredge the oysters in bread crumbs; fry briefly in remaining bacon fat. Return bacon to skillet. Crack the dozen eggs over everything. Over medium-high heat, with a spatula turn and stir until the eggs and the oysters have set.

Set the skillet in front of the hungry miner or on your table. It will serve one hungry miner or four hungry adults for breakfast, lunch, or dinner. And don't even *think* about the cholesterol.

Variations:

Some people like to add chopped onions, chopped peppers (any kind), and various other herbs and spices.

If you really feel you need a side dish with this, serve **Cabin Fried Potatoes** (page 52).

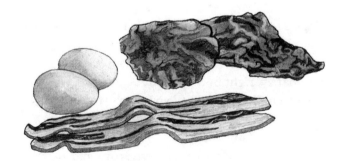

Ham and Red-Eye Gravy

This, like a few other recipes in this book, is not original, but because it fits so perfectly into the cast-iron mold, it needs to be included.

1 slice of ham about ¾ inch thick (12 to 16 ounces)
½ cup water
1 cup strong coffee

Pour water into #8 cast-iron skillet; bring to boil. Throw in ham slice. Cook, turning once, until water has almost evaporated. Remove ham from skillet; set aside.

Deglaze the skillet with the coffee. Put the ham back in the skillet and reduce the liquid by one-half.

You now have ham and red-eye gravy. Serve immediately, right in the skillet, or cover and it will hold on a back burner until you finish your side dishes.

Serves 2, but this is an easy recipe to expand to accommodate any number.

Goes well with **Cabin Fried Potatoes** and eggs, and either **Corn Bread, Mountain Bread,** or **Skillet Biscuits** (page 134) to slop up the juices.

Creekside

This is one of our favorite breakfast dishes up at the ranch, though it can work for lunch or dinner. It takes its name from the appearance of the finished product, which looks amazingly like the rocky side of a creek.

Cabin Fried Potatoes, page 52
ground meat or sausage of almost any variety
5 eggs
salt and pepper to taste
1 medium onion, cut medium dice
1 green bell pepper, cut medium dice

After you have cooked the Cabin Fried Potatoes, set aside. Throw the meat in the skillet. I particularly like bulk Italian sausage in this recipe, but just about any type of ground meat will work. Add onion and green pepper.

Brown the meat. Pour off excess fat. Toss the potatoes back in the skillet. Mix well with a spatula.

You are now in a holding pattern. This can be kept in the oven or served as soon as you ring the dinner bell.

Make sure everyone's ready to sit down, then crack eggs and throw in. Stir until eggs are set. Salt and pepper to taste. Serve in skillet.

Warm plates are a good idea. Serves 4.

Serve with Worcestershire, ketchup, Tabasco, horseradish, and mustard available. No tellin' what condiments your crew is going to want to top it off with. I have a friend who puts mustard on *everything*.

Toasted **Mountain Bread** goes well with this. See page 130.

Crow 'n Bear Porridge

Like the bear, this porridge is opportunistic. Start with oats, but after that, use whatever comes to hand. The dried fruits provide the sweetening, and the yogurts provide the cooling milky liquid; butter would be hyperexic, but serve what suits you.

2 cups old-fashioned oats
½ cup seeds: sunflower, flaxseed, whatever
¼ cup chopped nuts: walnut, almond, whatever
¼ cup dried fruit: blueberries, cranberries, etc.
6 cups water
pinch of salt

Combine all ingredients in a large saucepan. Bring to hard boil, turn down to slow boil, and keep on stirring until it feels like porridge, about 5 to 7 minutes.

Serve with an assortment of fruit-flavored yogurts, one per customer. Serves 6. Save any leftovers for the bear.

Lamb Kidneys and Fried Tomatoes

Credit our British heritages for this one. Broiled tomatoes are the perfect accompaniment to breakfast meats, but we'll use our well-seasoned cast iron skillet and pan-broil these.

4 lamb (or goat) kidneys, split, deveined,
   and cut in 1" chunks
salt and pepper
2 tablespoons butter
1 cup homemade beef stock OR
   1 can consommé, undiluted
1 tablespoon cornstarch, moistened in ¼ cup water
4 slices bread, sourdough or **City Bread** or
   Mountain Bread, toasted and cut in triangles
1 teaspoon canola oil
2 large slicing tomatoes, cut in half crosswise

Dry kidney pieces thoroughly on paper towel. If you will be using your good homemade beef stock, salt and pepper the pieces of lamb or goat kidneys. (If you must use consommé, don't salt the kidneys. A little pepper will suffice.)

In a #8 cast iron skillet over medium-hot flame, heat butter just until sizzling. Sauté kidney pieces, a few at a time, just until they turn grey. Do not overcook. Remove all kidney pieces from skillet and take skillet off heat.

Into the skillet pour the beef stock or consommé, stirring to incorporate the fond, if any. Return skillet to heat and add diluted cornstarch. Over medium heat, stir as the stock thickens. Add extra water if necessary to keep from congealing; you want this to be the consistency of a nice Thanksgiving gravy.

Return kidney pieces to skillet and heat thoroughly over low heat.

In a second skillet, heat canola oil but don't let it smoke. Add tomato halves to skillet, cut sides down, and sauté until they begin to shrivel.

Serve kidneys and sauce over toast points with tomato slices on the side. Serves 2 generously.

Maple Puffs

If you have an old-fashioned cast iron muffin pan, the fluted kind one might use for corn bread muffins, these delightful little puffs will turn out looking like small pumpkins. Light and delicately delicious, they make a lovely breakfast pastry,

2 eggs
2 tablespoons melted butter
½ cup light sour cream
2 tablespoons maple syrup
2 tablespoons brown sugar
1 teaspoon vanilla
½ cup flour
1 teaspoon baking soda

In a medium-sized bowl, beat eggs until light and fluffy. Stir in melted butter (cooled to room temperature), sour cream, maple syrup, brown sugar, and vanilla. Beat until well blended and light. In a second bowl, sift flour with baking soda, then add to first mixture, stirring until well blended.

Brush canola oil into a shaped, cast iron muffin pan, if you are fortunate enough to own one. Otherwise, use ordinary muffin pans.

Place empty pan in oven and preheat to 475 degrees. Remove pan from oven. Fill each hole to about ¾ of its capacity with thin batter. As these bake, they rise somewhat like popovers, though they do not become hollow at the center, but instead stay of a consistently light and puffy character.

Bake at 475 for 9 to 10 minutes, or until tops are puffy and lightly browned.

Remove puffs from pan and cool, inverted so the fluted part is on top (if using the old-fashioned fluted muffin tin). The product will remind you of a miniature pumpkin. As it cools, each puff will develop a small depression where the pumpkin's stem would be. Spoon a half teaspoon of jam into each depression.

Makes 15.

Strawberry Macadamia Scones

These crispy-crumbly scones, easy to assemble and packed with flavor (though not really "sweet"), will disappear quickly. If you don't have coconut milk, you can substitute Nestle's Media Crema, or half-and-half, or even evaporated milk. But try them first with canned coconut milk, if you can find it. (Look in the Thai/Asiatic food section of your supermarket.) The flavor is worth the search.

1 cup unbleached all-purpose flour
2 teaspoons baking powder
½ teaspoon sea salt
¼ cup turbinado (raw) sugar
4 tablespoons butter, room temperature
½ cup canned coconut milk
¼ cup macadamia nuts, minced fine
¼ cup dried strawberries, minced fine

In a medium-sized mixing bowl, sift or thoroughly stir together the flour, baking powder, salt, and sugar. Cut in the butter, then mix with your fingers until you've achieved fine crumbs. Stir in the coconut milk, mixing thoroughly. Add nuts and strawberries and stir to blend well. Dough will be wet and shaggy.

Turn out onto a generously floured board and knead a few quick strokes, incorporating flour until dough is manageable and no longer feels wet. Don't overwork the dough. Roll out lightly. You should have a square about 8 by 8 inches and about ½-inch thick.

Cut into 4 (or 8) equal pieces. Place in an ungreased #10 (12-inch) cast iron skillet. Bake at 400° for 26–28 minutes, or until golden brown. Remove skillet from oven, then remove scones to rack to cool. Split and spread with strawberry jam, if you like, or just eat as is. Makes 4 large scones or 8 small ones.

Some lunches you sit down to; others you pick up and go.
Some lunches you invite guests to; others you eat alone.
Some lunches can expand into a dinner; others are glorified snacks.
Some are soups, some are sandwiches, some are salads.
And some are elegant works of art.

Here's a little of each of these. Most of them see a cast iron skillet at least once.

Tangy Albacore Salad

This tuna salad eschews mayonnaise in favor of a savory green-and-black olive mix. It would be equally delightful made with shrimp instead of albacore.

3 stalks celery
2 medium tomatoes
1 (16-oz.) can water-packed albacore, drained
or 1 (16-oz.) can shrimp, drained
½ cup chopped black olives
½ cup muffuletta
spring greens

Garnish:

focaccia
olive oil
Parmesan cheese

Cut celery stalks in half lengthwise, then slice paper-thin. Cut tomato into fine dice. In a medium-sized bowl, mix celery, black olives, muffuletta, and tomato.

Add albacore or shrimp; toss to mix well. Serve on bed of mixed spring greens. For the garnish, split focaccia as you would an English muffin. Toast focaccia pieces, cut into points, drizzle with olive oil, and sprinkle with Parmesan cheese. Serve alongside the salad. Serves 4.

Fish Tacos

Some years ago, Jim Morehouse set up a fish taco booth at the Arcata Oyster Festival. Soon he had sold all his fish and people were still standing in line, so he sent out for more fish and just kept the tacos coming. This is an adaptation of the recipe that made such a hit that day, cooked on Coleman stoves in large skillets. He brought the original version back from San Felipe.

For one dozen fish tacos:

4 eggs
1 quart milk
2 pounds fish filet, any firm white fish
2–3 cups canola oil
3 cups panko crumbs
1 dozen corn tortillas
mayonnaise
1 small head cabbage, sliced fine
2 cups salsa
3 limes, cut into six wedges each

Beat together eggs and milk in a medium-size mixing bowl. Cut fish into 1" cubes and place in the egg/milk mixture. Set aside. In your largest cast iron skillet—at least a 10"–12" one—pour in about ¾ inch canola oil. Heat to just barely smoking.

Put panko crumbs into a plastic bag. Put in half the fish and shake to coat. Place coated fish into hot oil. Cook no more than 30 seconds; turn and cook another 30 seconds. With pluckers, remove cooked fish. Set on paper towels to drain.

When all the fish has been cooked in this manner, briefly heat tortillas over an open flame, a few seconds on each side. Off the heat, hold each tortilla in your palm and coat with mayonnaise. Add about three or four pieces of cooked fish to tortilla. Sprinkle shredded cabbage over fish. Add a tablespoon of salsa and a squeeze of lime juice.

Set out extra wedges of lime and extra salsa and/or hot sauce and serve immediately. Serves 4.

From the fish taco recipe you may have leftover batter. After all the fish is out of the skillet and while the oil is still hot, drop in tablespoons of the leftover batter. Let them cook, turning, until brown on all sides. Remove from oil and let cool. Toss them to your dog and say, "Hush, puppy."

We have three cooking oils on our *mise en place*: olive oil, canola oil, and peanut oil. Olive oil is for quick, medium-temperature sautéing. Canola oil can take higher browning temperatures without burning. For small batches of hot, heavy-duty browning, such as stir-frying, peanut oil is best, despite its expense, because it can stand the highest heat.

Indonesian-Style Lettuce Wraps

This messy, festive, help-yourself tasting party gives new meaning to "hands-on." Consider providing moist towels, finger bowls, or those little foil-wrapped towelettes. Kids love making their own.

½ cup white vinegar
2 tablespoons turbinado sugar
2 (2") crosswise chunks of peeled cucumber
dash pepper
2 tablespoons peanut oil
½ large boneless, skinless chicken breast, cut in
   ½-inch dice
2 tablespoons soy sauce or Terikayi sauce
½ to ¾ cup jicama, cut tiny dice
½ large sweet red pepper, cut small dice
10–12 cubes candied ginger, minced
1 cup peanut sauce
12–16 large leaves green leaf lettuce

First, in a small, flat dish combine vinegar and sugar, stirring until sugar is dissolved. Cut each 2" crosswise slice of cucumber lengthwise into skinny matchsticks. Marinate in vinegar/sugar mixture. Sprinkle dash of pepper over all. Set aside.

In a large cast iron skillet, heat peanut oil over medium flame. Quickly stir-fry chicken dice just until slightly browned—don't overdo it or they'll toughen up. Drain and remove to small bowl. Pour soy sauce over and toss to blend, then pour off excess soy sauce. Either serve in this small bowl or transfer to a small serving bowl.

Find separate small bowls—teacups will do, if you have nothing else—for the cucumber in marinade, the diced jicama, the diced sweet red pepper, and the candied ginger. You can serve the peanut sauce right from the jar or put it also in a small separate bowl. Present lettuce leaves in a large bowl.

Diners use the lettuce leaves to assemble their choice of fillings upon, then, rolling up the edges of the leaves, they eat the crisp-crunchy-succulent-sour-sweet packages, usually amid laughter and with rolled eyes.

This would ideally be accompanied by warm, homemade naan, but if you have none, try warming a pita pocket on a hot skillet in the same manner used for **Skillet Pockets** (page 22).

These proportions would serve about 4, but obviously this is an expandable feast.

Ham and Cheese Skillet Pockets

Quick, easy, and tasty: a lunch you can take with you to eat out of hand. Not as messy as a sandwich, either. This recipe serves one; scale up for more servings.

For each serving:

1 pita pocket (Mediterranean-style bread)
3 very thin slices deli ham
1 tablespoon **Honey Mustard Dressing**
¼ cup canned sliced mushrooms (or less)
¼ cup baby spinach
2 very thin slices sweet red onion
2 slices Jarlsberg or Swiss cheese (deli sliced)

Carefully slice open pita pocket, cutting only in a semicircle, not all the way apart. Stack the ham slices and spread with **Honey Mustard Dressing,** p. 122. On top of the ham, layer the mushrooms, spinach, onion, and cheese. Use a spatula to help you slide this package inside the pita pocket. Be sure all edges of the cheese are tucked inside.

Heat a #5 cast iron skillet until, when you hold your palms over it, it warms them. Do the same with a handled pot of such a size as to fit neatly into the #5. Keep the heat going under the skillet.

Now, with the spatula, slide pita pocket into the hot skillet and immediately top the pita pocket with the bottom of the heated pot, pressing down for about 2 minutes or until cheese is melted. Set aside in warming oven while you prepare the rest of the pockets.

Variation:

Greek Skillet Pockets

Follow same method as Mexican Skillet Pockets (facing page), but fill with 1 cup ground lamb, browned and drained; a thick layer of good hummus, 2 tablespoons pine nuts; 1 tablespoon fresh mint leaves, chopped; and feta cheese, crumbled.

Mexican Skillet Pockets

This serves one. Scale up all ingredients to serve more.

ground beef, about ⅓ pound
1 pita pocket, at room temperature
1 cup canned chili beans, drained
1½ canned peeled green chiles
2 teaspoons chopped cilantro (if desired)
3 deli slices Monterey jack or Cheddar cheese

Cut a circle of aluminum foil the size of the bottom of a #3 cast iron skillet. Set aside. With a long, sharp knife cut a horizontal slit halfway around the pita pocket. Do not cut farther than halfway.

Now, in a #3 skillet, shape raw ground beef into a patty, of uniform size, that fills the skillet. Fry over medium-high heat until bottom is slightly browned. Using spatula and keeping patty in one piece, turn only once and slightly brown bottom of patty. Carefully lift patty out (try to keep it still in one piece) and place on circle of aluminum foil.

Cover with a uniform layer of drained chili beans. Top beans with peeled green chiles, spread open. Sprinkle cilantro over chiles. Top all with slices of cheese.

Sliding spatula beneath the aluminum foil circle, coax beef/beans/chile/cheese stack into pocket in pita bread. Pull out aluminum foil circle.

Heat a #5 cast iron skillet to nearly smoking. Also heat a handled pot of a size to fit neatly inside the #5 skillet. Place pita pocket in hot skillet, place hot handled pot on top of pita pocket, and press down until cheese melts—about 2 minutes.

Remove from skillet and serve immediately.

Accompany with fresh pico de gallo and beverage of your choice. If possible, serve with Sidral, a refreshing Mexican bottled sparkling cider (non-alcoholic).

Peanut Butter, Bacon, and Dill Pickle Sandwich on Rye

I've been making this sandwich for years. I know it sounds more than a little strange, but try it once and you'll be hooked.

Some years ago I was in an elk camp high in the Colorado Rockies. At about 4:30 in the morning we were all standing around in the cook tent trying to get warm and get something into our bellies for the morning hunt. The cook had a big cast-iron skillet of bacon frying on the camp stove. There was toast available, and in the larder I spotted a jar of peanut butter and some dill pickles. Without telling anyone what I was doing, I slapped together this sandwich and started munching on it.

"What the hell is that?" asked the other hunters. When I told them, they turned up their noses and wanted no part of it, saying it sounded terrible.

But one of the more adventurous sports said he'd give it a try, so I slapped together a sandwich for him. He sank his teeth into it and said, "Hey, this is pretty good." Before long, everyone was munching on this sandwich.

You owe it to yourself to at least try it.

To make 4 sandwiches:

1 pound bacon, any style, cooked the way you like it
8 slices rye bread, toasted (any other bread will work)
2 whole dill pickles, sliced lengthwise
1 cup peanut butter, any style

To make one sandwich, spread peanut butter on 2 slices of warm, toasted bread. Top one piece of toast with bacon and pickle slices. Top with other piece of toast and serve.

That's it.

Crow 'n Bear Frittata

Named for our ranch in the mountains, this dish takes cast iron wrists to turn the two skillets. You may want to use a light-weight frittata pan, the kind with hinges.

1 cup dried sliced potatoes
1¼ cup boiling water
¼ cup sundried tomatoes, chopped
1 cup baby spinach, chopped
2 sweet Italian sausages, cut in ¼-inch slices
½ small onion, sliced fine
½ cup shredded Parmesan cheese
¼ cup olive oil
4 eggs, beaten light

In a small bowl, pour 1 cup boiling water over dried potatoes and let stand for 20 minutes. Pour ¼ cup boiling water over sundried tomatoes and let soak. Remove potatoes, drain, and dry on a sheet of paper towel. Put spinach in the potato water to wilt.

Meanwhile, in one #8 cast iron skillet, brown the sausage slices, set to one side of the skillet, add the sliced onions and stir until golden, stirring up the sausage fond with a spatula. Set aside.

Heat a second #8 skillet over a medium flame; when skillet is hot, add half the olive oil, swirling to distribute. Fry potatoes until golden, stirring as necessary. Now add the sausage and onion mixture. Sprinkle Parmesan evenly over the mixture. Add wilted spinach. Turn the burner down a little and keep this skillet over the flame.

Heat the first skillet (now empty) over a medium flame and add the remainder of the olive oil, swirling to distribute. In the second skillet, pour beaten eggs over the other ingredients. Cook as you would an omelet, lifting the edge of the mixture to let uncooked eggs flow under. Let it cook until light golden (peek under an edge), then pour off any excess oil from the first skillet and invert over the second skillet. Holding both handles together, flip the skillets so the first one is on the bottom. Let cook another minute. Serve immediately.

Serves 2 really hungry adults or 4 picky children.

Garlic Black Beans

Everybody has a favorite bean recipe. This is ours. I don't soak my beans; I just cook 'em a little longer. They're not as likely to burst open if they're not soaked.

This makes an excellent lunch dish. With variations, bump it up into the dinner category.

3 cups black beans
4 to 5 quarts water
¼ pound salt pork cut medium dice (¼-inch cubes)
1 medium head garlic, with cloves separated, peeled, and crushed
2 medium onions, diced fine
6 sweet baby peppers, cut medium dice
1 tablespoon olive oil
2 teaspoons cumin, or to taste
1 teaspoon white vinegar
salt and pepper to taste
1 bunch fresh cilantro, chopped fine

Bring beans to boil in a large (6-quart) pot. Reduce heat to a slow rolling boil. Cook until *al dente*. Depending on the age and state of your beans, this could be anywhere from an hour to 2 or 3 hours.

While beans are boiling, try out salt pork in a cast iron skillet. Set aside. Sauté garlic, onions, and baby peppers in olive oil. Sauté briefly until onions are translucent. Remove from skillet; set aside with salt pork.

When beans are cooked to your taste, remove and strain 1 cup of the black beans from the large pot. Put strained beans in skillet; mash with potato masher or large spoon. Throw vegetables and salt pork back in skillet with the mashed beans. Add cumin. Cook and stir briefly over low heat to combine flavors.

Strain the beans that remain in the pot, reserving the water for use in stock- or bread-making. Off the fire, return the strained beans to the cooking pot. Add contents of skillet (vegetable-and-mashed bean mixture) to the strained beans in the large pot. Stir to mix well. Stir in vinegar.

Turn beans into a ceramic serving dish. They are now in a holding pattern. They can be kept warm in the oven until ready for use, or, for extra flavor, can be held in the refrigerator and reheated the next day. When ready to serve, taste the beans and add salt and pepper to taste, if necessary. Then sprinkle with chopped cilantro. Serves 6 to 8 as a side dish, 4 to 6 as a main dish with sausages (see Variations).

Variations:

This dish goes very well with linguica or just about any other large sausage. Cook sausage separately in a skillet, then cut diagonally and add to beans just before serving.

Also excellent with smoked ham hocks. Allow one hock per serving. Boil hocks, let cool, remove meat from bones, remove skin and excess fat. Cut meat into large dice and throw into bean pot. Pat skins dry and fry in skillet to make cracklings for your lucky dog.

Accompaniments:

Corn Bread (page 132) or **Skillet Biscuits** (page 134) and a green salad make this a complete dinner. Beer goes well with this dish.

Stuffed Breast of Veal

This dish can be the centerpiece for an elegant summertime patio luncheon or extravagant picnic.

1 (3-pound) breast of veal
salt and pepper
1 package frozen spinach or chard, thawed and
    drained
1 medium carrot, small dice
1 medium onion, small dice
1 stalk celery, sliced and diced small
1 tablespoon dried parsley or cilantro
4 cloves garlic crushed, peeled, cut small dice
¼ cup olive oil
2 beef bullets (page 68)
1 cup dry white wine or vermouth
1 cup bread crumbs
1 tablespoon Italian seasoning
1 raw egg
fresh rosemary sprigs

Cut a pocket in the breast of veal, beginning at the large end. You might want to have your butcher do this if you're not handy with a filet knife. Rub inside of pocket with salt and pepper.

In a cast iron skillet, briefly sauté all vegetables, including spinach, in olive oil. Add beef bullets and a splash or two of the wine. Cover and simmer until vegetables are just tender. Stir in bread crumbs and Italian seasoning.

Remove from heat. Stir in egg. Spoon into pocket in veal breast. Sew edges together with kitchen twine. Rub veal with oil. Place on rack in cast iron Dutch oven. Add remaining wine. Roast, covered, in oven preheated to 350 degrees for about 15–20 minutes.

Reduce heat to 275 degrees. Continue cooking for 1½ to 2 hours. Check after 1 hour. When internal temperature of breast has reached 140+ degrees, uncover and place Dutch oven under broiler for about 5 minutes. Keep your eye on it so it doesn't char.

Set veal aside to cool on rack. Chill overnight in refrigerator. Slice and serve cold on chilled plates.

Garnish each plate with a sprig of fresh rosemary. Serves 4 to 6, depending on size of veal breast and heartiness of side dishes.

Variations:

You can substitute breast of lamb for the veal, but it will not be nearly as satisfying. This is because the bones in the breast of veal, not yet having fully formed, are mostly cartilage, which means you can eat them. They provide an unexpected toothiness, a welcome, savory, meaty crunch.

Accompaniments:

A good quality store-bought sourdough bread and thin slices of Parmesan or other hard cheeses such as Romano or a dry Monterey Jack. For a truly elegant meal, serve a cold soup such as gazpacho or vichyssoise. Serve with **Asian Pear and Fig** or **Bosc and Brie** salad.

Wine Recommendations:

This dish is especially good with a chilled Pinot Grigio or dry Riesling.

Lunches

Minestrone

As with chili, there are thousands of recipes for minestrone. In fact, minestrone simply means "big soup" in Italian. Here is one recipe; use it as a guide only and let your own creative juices flow into this soup. This is a meal in itself. I always make a lot of minestrone because it is labor intensive and it freezes very well.

½ cup dry white beans
2 quarts water
4 tablespoons olive oil
1 cup potatoes, cut medium dice
1 rutabaga, cut medium dice
2 carrots, cut medium dice
1 large green pepper, cut medium dice
2 stalks celery, thinly sliced
2 medium onions, cut medium dice
1 medium leek, sliced and diced
¼ pound salt pork, medium dice
2 cans stewed Italian-style tomatoes
1 bay leaf
½ cup small pasta such as shells, rotini, bowties, etc.

1 quart chicken stock
2 tablespoons fresh basil, chopped
1 tablespoon fresh parsley, chopped

Cook beans in water at a low rolling boil until just barely tender. Drain and set aside. Reserve water beans have cooked in.

In a large cast iron skillet, add olive oil and all the vegetables except the tomatoes. Sauté over low heat until onions are just barely translucent. Cover and turn heat to dead low.

In a small cast iron skillet, try out salt pork. Then lightly brown salt pork in the same skillet. Add salt pork to vegetable mixture. Throw everything into an 8-quart stock pot. Include tomatoes, bay leaf, and pasta.

Now is the time to cut loose with some of your good chicken stock. Add a quart to the stockpot. If you don't have or don't want to use your good chicken stock, it is certainly acceptable to use store-bought low-sodium chicken broth in this recipe.

Add additional water—you can use the reserved bean water—to bring contents up to about 6 or 7 quarts. Bring to a boil, stirring occasionally with a wooden spoon. Reduce heat to a simmer and cook until pasta is *al dente*.

Adjust seasoning and serve garnished with fresh basil and parsley and any other Italian herbs that come to hand from your garden. Serve immediately with crumbled Parmesan cheese and slices of your fresh homemade bread. Serves 10 to 12.

This dish will improve considerably if allowed to cool and rest overnight in your refrigerator. Reheat before serving.

Some Folks Like Cheese in Their Minestrone

During my childhood my grampa lived with us, off and on. I noticed that one of his favorite pastimes was making minestrone. It seems as if there was always a large pot of it simmering on a back burner.

I was never quite sure of most of the ingredients, but of one I was very aware. You see, near serving time, Gramps would toss in a few chunks of aged Parmesan cheese.

When the soup was ladled out, I always considered myself fortunate if I found, in my bowl, a chunk of that Parmesan hiding among the pasta and vegetables.

Scotch Broth

Remember the bone you saved from the joint of lamb you used for your **Lamb and Bamb** *dinner? (p. 84) You need it now. This dish freezes very well, so it makes sense to cook up a lot and freeze leftovers.*

1 bone from a leg of lamb
1 cup dried barley
4 quarts water
2 tablespoons canola oil
leftover lamb scraps, 2 cups or more
2 medium onions, small dice
2 medium carrots, medium dice
2 stalks celery, sliced and diced small
1 small turnip or rutabaga, cut small dice
6 cloves garlic, peeled and cut small dice
1 teaspoon salt
½ teaspoon coarse ground black pepper

In a large saucepan add barley and lamb bone to water. Bring to boil, reduce to simmer, and let cook, uncovered, until barley is tender, about an hour or so.

While barley and lamb bone are cooking, heat canola oil in a cast iron skillet and sauté remaining ingredients, including lamb scraps. Sauté until onions turn translucent.

Transfer contents of sauté pan to the soup pot. Continue to cook at a low simmer for another 15 to 20 minutes. Remove from heat. Remove lamb bone.

You can serve now, but this soup will improve dramatically if it's allowed to cool and spend the night in the refrigerator.

Reheat before serving. Serves 8 generously.

Abalone Chowder

Most people feed the abalone trimmings to the seagulls. I can tell you that's a mistake, because they make a truly excellent chowder, better than most clam chowders. This will not look especially appetizing, because the abalone trimmings are black in color and throw off a somewhat unappealing inky effluvium similar to that emitted by squid. Don't let this put you off; just judge by the flavor.

¾ pound abalone trimmings, cut medium dice
¼ pound salt pork, cut medium dice
3 medium potatoes, peeled and cut medium dice
2 medium onions, cut medium dice
2 carrots, cut small dice
2 stalks celery, sliced and diced fine
8 cloves garlic, peeled and cut small dice
2 tablespoons butter
4 quarts water

In a small cast iron skillet, try out salt pork. In a large cast iron skillet over medium heat, gently sauté potatoes, onions, carrots, celery, and garlic in butter.

Throw in abalone trimmings and tried salt pork and continue on heat.

Bring water to boil in a cast iron Dutch oven. If you're close to the ocean—and you should be—throw in 2 cups of ocean water. This will lend a most exquisite flavor.

Pour contents of skillet into the boiling water in the Dutch oven. Cover and let simmer until abalone is *al dente*. This may take 3 to 4 hours. Check occasionally and add liquid if necessary. Serves 6.

This goes well with **Abalone Steaks** (page 109).

Variations:

This recipe might also be prepared with large, fresh-caught clams chopped medium. I've personally never done it with clams, though I suspect it might work. If you try it, please let us know how it turns out.

Split Pea Soup

Some people like a very thick split pea soup. This recipe can be thickened by reducing or by adding a thickening agent such as cornstarch or arrowroot dissolved in cold water.

**2 meaty smoked ham hocks or enough to make a
   pound of cooked lean meat**
2 medium carrots, chopped fine dice
1 medium onion, chopped fine dice
1 stalk celery, sliced and diced fine
6 cloves garlic crushed, peeled, and diced small
2 tablespoons olive oil
3–4 quarts cold water
2 cups split peas
salt and pepper

Boil ham hocks in water to cover for 20 to 30 minutes. Remove and let cool. Cut off skin and exterior fat.

In a large (8 quart) cast iron bean pot (if you're lucky enough to have one) or an ordinary stockpot, briefly sauté vegetables in olive oil. Pour in about 3 to 4 quarts cold water. Add split peas and defatted ham hocks, along with the bones. Bring to a rolling boil. Reduce to simmer. Cook until peas are tender. Remove ham hocks; set aside.

Pull out and drain about 1 cup of the pea/vegetable mixture. Mash with potato masher. Return to pot to thicken soup. Salt and pepper to taste. Strip meat from ham hock bones; chop into medium dice and return to pot.

Can be served immediately, but flavor will improve if held in refrigerator overnight and reheated. Serves 6 to 8.

Variations:

For color, use 1 cup green split peas and 1 cup yellow split peas.

For an elegant touch, stir in a teaspoon of sherry into each portion as you serve it. Top with sour cream and chives. This comes close to being a full meal.

Considering cookie-making, a few words:

Keep the process simple. You don't need a mixer, a sifter, or a lot of bowls to make good cookies. I cream my butter with a kitchen fork, sift dry ingredients with my fingers, and do all my stirring with a wooden spoon. And I use an ulu or a chef's knife to chop nuts (the ulu is more manageable), which simplifies clean-up.

In most cases, one medium-size mixing bowl is all you'll need. If assembly and clean-up doesn't feel like such a chore, you're likely to bake more cookies for your family to enjoy. And if the equipment and the process are kept simple, even kids can get involved in cookie-making.

Improvise. You can make distinctive, attractive butter cookies without a cookie press. Just roll the dough between your palms to make little balls, place in an ungreased iron skillet (or on an ungreased cookie sheet), and flatten with the bottom of a tumbler dipped in whatever kind of sugar or sugar/flour mixture strikes your fancy. Then search your kitchen for whatever will make a distinctive impression on the tops of the flattened cookies. I have successfully used a fork, a potato ricer, a ravioli wheel, and the bottom of a cut-glass tumbler. (Kids will love this part of the process.)

Strive for the healthful. We prefer a less-sweet cookie because, to be frank about it, we can eat more of them. Also, a cookie not overladen with sweetener tastes better, to us, as an any-time-of-the-day snack.

With most of these cookies, the flavor tends to build as you chew and then come out, in its full delicious flowering, as an aftertaste that will lead you right back for another. We prefer this dynamic to the highly sugared product that hits you in the face and after one or two (depending upon your susceptibility) sends you into sugar-shock.

Speaking of sugar, you won't find the traditional refined white sugar in our kitchen. Instead, we use raw or turbinado sugar, which hasn't had all the nutrition milled out of it and to us tastes better. Ditto brown sugar: we go for the least-processed product we can find, with the highest content of original molasses remaining from the sugar cane. Again, to our palates it makes tastier cookies. And there's much to be said for barley malt syrup or just plain old molasses.

As for the shortening, I always use a little real butter, for its superior flavor and because I prefer an honest, old-fashioned saturated fat to a synthetic trans-fat. (Needless to say, there is no Crisco or margarine in our kitchen.) But I do cut the amount by half and substitute, for the remainder of the shortening, light sour cream, Neufchatel cheese, or a high-quality olive oil. This strategy reduces calories and boosts flavor.

Light sour cream and Neufchatel cheese (which tastes and handles just like cream cheese but with one-third less calories) both convey a subtle cheesecake-type flavor that plays off especially well against dried fruits and nuts. They also provide essential calcium, so you can prescribe yourself a cookie now and then without feeling guilty.

These are the kinds of cookies you can proudly present in a tin at Christmastime, but they are also the kinds to slip by the dozen into the bib of your overalls, to sustain you through a long day on the tractor.

Anise Claws

For a less sweet cookie, omit the powdered sugar at the end.

4 tablespoons butter
4 tablespoons olive oil
½ cup turbinado sugar
1 tablespoon anise seed
1 cup flour
½ cup powdered sugar

Cream butter, add olive oil a little at a time, then add sugar and beat until well blended. Add anise seed; mix well. Add 1 cup flour and stir till blended. Take up a tablespoon of dough, roll it into a ball between your palms, then shape into a crescent, place on ungreased cookie sheet, and crimp the top with a fork. Proceed in this manner until dough is all used up. Bake in preheated 325 degree oven for 30 minutes. While cookies are still warm, roll in powdered sugar, then set aside to cool. Makes 18.

Black Walnut Thumbprints

The flavor unfolds by the second bite; then it's hard to stop.

4 tablespoons butter
¼ cup light sour cream
½ cup turbinado sugar
1 teaspoon natural black walnut flavor
½ cup ground walnuts, whirled in coffee grinder
1½ cup unbleached flour
30 walnut halves

Cream butter, add sour cream and beat till well blended. Add sugar, beat again. Add black walnut flavor; stir till well blended. Add ground walnuts, crumbling between your fingers to break up any small lumps; mix well. Add flour, mix well, turn out on floured board and knead a few times to form one cohesive lump. Pinch off dough by tablespoons and roll between your palms to make a ball. Place on ungreased cookie sheet and make a thumbprint in the middle of the ball. Put a walnut half in the thumbprint. Bake in preheated 325 degree oven for 25 minutes. Remove to rack to cool. Makes 30.

Ginger Sandies

These slightly crumbly cookies have a delicate crunch. They're probably too fragile to travel well, but since they disappear so quickly, we may never find out.

8 tablespoons butter
8 tablespoons olive oil
½ cup brown sugar
2 eggs
2 cups flour
4 tablespoons dry milk powder
2 teaspoons baking powder
3 teaspoons lime juice (can use lemon)
⅔ cup candied ginger, chopped fine
⅔ cup walnuts, chopped fine

Cream butter, beat in olive oil a little at a time, beat in brown sugar, beat in eggs.

Sift flour, powdered milk, and baking powder together; add to batter and stir to mix well. Add lime juice; mix until well blended. Add ginger and walnuts. Stir to mix.

Drop by heaping tablespoonsful into well-seasoned, ungreased iron skillets (two 12" skillets will accommodate the batch), or use nonstick cookie sheets if you don't have skillets. Cookies will spread out to about a 3" diameter as they cook, so leave at least 1" space between them.

Bake for 30 minutes at 350°. These aromatic drop cookies will be an even, medium brown on the bottoms and edges, but only lightly browned on the tops. Remove cookies from iron skillets or cookie sheets and allow to cool on rack. Makes 32–36.

Lemony Black-Eyed Susans

Aromatic and flavorful, these lemony pressed cookies have a chewy texture and a tangy aftertaste that calls out for another.

¼ cup butter, softened
4 tablespoons Neufchatel cheese, softened
½ cup turbinado sugar
1 teaspoon lemon extract
2 tablespoons concentrated lemon juice
½ cup sweetened baker's coconut
24 dried cherries
¼ cup dark rum

Soak dried cherries in rum. While cherries are soaking, in a medium-sized bowl cream butter with fork, add softened Neufchatel cheese, and beat together with wooden spoon. One by one, add sugar, lemon extract, and lemon juice, stirring well after adding each. Stir in baker's coconut and flour, mixing thoroughly.

Take up dough by rounded tablespoons and shape into balls by rolling between palms.

Place on ungreased cookie sheet, leaving at least an inch between balls. Flatten with a tumbler bottom dipped in a small amount of flour and sugar. Score lightly to resemble petals of a flower OR put dough through cookie press, selecting a disk shaped like a daisy.

In the center of each "flower" put one soaked, drained cherry.

Bake in preheated 325 oven 18 to 20 minutes or until cookies are lightly browned. Remove cookie sheet from oven and let cool to the touch before removing cookies with a spatula. Makes 24.

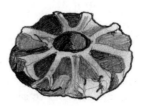

Maple Bear Claweds

These cookies go together easily, requiring only one mixing bowl, a fork, and a wooden spoon. Not too fatty, not too sweet, they have a flavor that lingers. Watch your resident bear come back for more.

4 tablespoons butter
¼ cup light sour cream
¼ cup unrefined dark brown sugar
¼ cup maple syrup
¼ cup dark rum
1 cup ground pecans, whirled in coffee grinder
1½ cup unbleached flour
½ cup pecan pieces, chopped fine
sweetened cocoa mix OR unsweetened cocoa
**   plus 2 tablespoons powdered sugar, mixed**

In a medium-sized mixing bowl, cream butter with a fork. Using a wooden spoon, beat in sour cream and brown sugar. Add maple syrup and stir to blend. Add ground pecans, stirring to blend. Add flour, then chopped pecans, stirring to blend well.

Take up batter by tablespoons and shape between palms into round balls. Place in ungreased cast iron skillet (or a heavy cookie sheet, if you must), leaving an inch between balls. Dip a tumbler's bottom into the sweetened cocoa mix and flatten each ball, refreshing tumbler bottom with cocoa mix every two balls or so. Score each flattened ball once with a fork dipped in cocoa mix, one way only. Do not crosshatch fork marks as you would for peanut butter cookies; you want this to look as if a tiny bear had clawed each cookie.

Bake in preheated 325-degree oven for 25 minutes. Remove to rack to cool. Makes about 36.

Pecan Blondies

Quick and easy—they use only one mixing bowl—these little cookies are crunchy, aromatic, and not too sweet.

4 tablespoons butter
½ cup sweetened condensed milk
¼ cup spiced rum
½ cup dried milk powder
1 cup unbleached all-purpose flour
¾ cup pecan pieces

Cream butter, then add sweetened condensed milk. Blend well. Stir in rum, mix again. Add dried milk powder and flour, stirring to blend well. Add pecan pieces, stir to mix. Place by flattened teaspoonfuls on generously greased, double-thick cookie sheet. Bake at 300 degrees for 20–25 minutes, or until the tops just begin to gently brown. Remove to rack to cool. Makes 3 dozen.

Pecan Brownies

4 tablespoons butter, softened
4 tablespoons olive oil
½ cup dark brown sugar
1 egg, beaten
1 tablet Mexican-style table chocolate, melted in double boiler
½ cup flour
¼ cup nonfat dry milk
1 teaspoon baking powder
1 cup chopped pecans

Cream butter, stir in olive oil a little at a time and beat to blend. Beat in brown sugar, then egg, then chocolate, beating all to blend well.

Sift flour together with dry milk and baking powder. Combine with wet ingredients, stirring until well blended. Stir in pecans. Fold batter into a greased, floured, 9-inch square glass baking pan.

Bake in preheated 375° oven about 20 minutes. Remove from heat and set aside to cool. When pan is at room temperature, cut into 2x2-inch bars. Makes about 16.

Rummy Cocoroons

Chewy, decadently rummy, and not too sweet, these cookies make a wonderful holiday or anytime treat. Watch your guests come back for more.

¼ pound butter
½ tablet Mexican chocolate, softened by warming
½ cup brown sugar
2 tablespoons molasses
2 tablespoons dark rum
1 cup flour
1 teaspoon baking powder
½ cup slivered almonds or pecans, chopped
¾ to 1 cup baker's coconut

Cream butter, add softened Mexican chocolate, beat to blend. Beat in brown sugar and molasses. Add rum and stir to blend.

Sift flour with baking powder. Add little by little to chocolate/butter mixture. Add nuts; stir to blend well.

To shape each cookie, take up a heaping teaspoonful of batter and roll it between your palms to make a ball.

Roll this ball in baker's coconut. Place in ungreased skillet. Leave an inch between cookies, since they will flatten out as they bake.

Bake in preheated 400 degree oven for 15–17 minutes, or until coconut begins to brown.

Remove from oven and let skillet cool on rack for about 5 minutes, then with a spatula carefully remove cookies to a wire rack to cool. Makes 24.

Spicy Pumpkin Cookies

¼ pound butter
¼ cup turbinado sugar
1 large egg, beaten
1½ cup canned pumpkin
2 tablespoons butterscotch topping
1 tablespoon molasses
1½ cup flour
2 teaspoons baking powder
2 teaspoons cinnamon
½ cup pecan pieces
½ cup candied ginger, chopped fine
½ cup dried cranberries (optional)

Cream butter, beat in sugar and egg, then add canned pumpkin, butterscotch topping, and molasses, and beat until well blended. Sift flour with baking powder and cinnamon. Add to the previous mixture and stir until well blended. Add pecan pieces, ginger, and cranberries (if you're using them); stir until blended.

   Drop by tablespoonfuls onto ungreased cookie sheet, leaving 1 inch between drops. Bake at 350 degrees for 30 minutes or until a toothpick inserted in center comes out clean. Remove cookies to rack to cool. Makes 36.

Strawberry Macadamia Cookies

¼ cup chopped dried strawberries
¼ cup rum
4 tablespoons butter, softened to room temperature
4 tablespoons Neufchatel cheese, softened
¼ cup turbinado sugar
¼ cup finely chopped macadamia nuts
¾ cup unbleached all-purpose flour

In a small glass, soak strawberries in rum for about an hour. Cream butter and Neufchatel cheese together. Stir in sugar and mix well. Drain strawberries and add to mix. Reserve rum for another dish; it will only get more flavorful.

Add macadamia nuts and stir to blend. Stir in flour and mix thoroughly. Take up dough by the tablespoon and roll between your palms to make a ball. Place balls on ungreased cookie sheet, leaving an inch on all sides. Flatten with a tumbler bottom dipped in sugar/flour mixture. Score with a ravioli wheel to make "tire tracks."

Bake cookies in a preheated 325-degree oven for 20 to 22 minutes or until bottoms are browned. Remove from cookie sheet and cool on rack. Makes 18.

Five-Spice Cookies

These aromatic, savory cookies look like little brown drain covers, but don't let that put you off: they just hold their sugar topping all the better for the grid marks.

4 tablespoons butter
4 tablespoons Neufchatel cheese
¼ cup dark brown sugar ("molasses sugar" is best)
1½ teaspoons Chinese 5-spice powder
1 tablespoon rum (use rum your dried strawberries
    have soaked in, if you have any)
¼ cup chopped pine nuts or cashews
¼ cup candied ginger, chopped fine
¾ cup unbleached all-purpose flour
2 teaspoons turbinado or raw sugar

Cream butter, add Neufchatel cheese and cream together. In succession add brown sugar, 5-spice powder, and rum, stirring to mix well after each addition. Stir in nuts and ginger, then add flour and stir until all is thoroughly mixed and no pockets of flour remain.

Take up by the tablespoonful and roll between your palms to make a ball. Place balls in ungreased iron skillet or on ungreased cookie sheet, leaving an inch between balls. Flatten with a tumbler bottom dipped in sugar/flour mixture; then, with a potato ricer, make impressions on each flattened cookie. Sprinkle turbinado or raw sugar over tops of cookies.

Bake in preheated 325-degree oven for 18 to 20 minutes or until bottoms are lightly browned. Remove from oven and cool 2 minutes in pan, then remove to wire rack to continue cooling. Makes 24.

Orange Cranberry Sunbursts

Not too sweet, slightly crunchy, with intense orange flavor, this cookie takes its shape from a pattern in the bottom of a Morehouse household beer stein. Look around your own home; you're sure to find interesting patterns on the bottoms of glassware, especially cut-glass stemware. You can rename this after your own favorite pattern.

4 tablespoons butter
4 tablespoons olive oil
½ cup turbinado sugar
1 tablespoon orange zest
3 teaspoons orange extract
½ teaspoon allspice
¼ cup juice fresh orange
1½ cups unbleached all-purpose flour
½ cup finely chopped walnuts
¼ cup dried cranberries, soaked in rum

Cream butter; gradually beat in olive oil. Add sugar; beat to blend. Add orange zest, orange extract, allspice, and fresh orange juice. Beat well.

Add flour a little at a time, stirring after each addition until thoroughly mixed. Add chopped walnuts.

Drain dried cranberries, reserving rum for another purpose. Add drained cranberries to mix. Stir all thoroughly until nuts and cranberries are evenly distributed throughout the batter and no patches of flour remain in the bottom or on the sides of the mixing bowl.

Take up by tablespoons and roll between your palms to make a ball. Place balls on large, ungreased, cast iron skillet, leaving an inch between balls on all sides.

Press patterned bottom of glassware into a small, flat dish containing a mix of ¼ cup flour, ¼ cup sugar. This will prevent its sticking to the cookie dough. (I keep a jar of this flour/sugar mix in my baking cabinet, to be used for just this purpose, since I make a lot of cookies.)

Now center the glassware over each ball of cookie dough and press down firmly. Carefully trim away any excess dough that squeezes out from under the edge of the glass. (Your kids will enjoy helping you with this.)

Bake in preheated 350-degree oven for 20 minutes, or until bottoms of cookies are lightly browned. Remove skillet from oven and remove cookies to cooling rack. Makes 22–24.

Note:

Although all the cookies in this book were made in cast iron skillets, if you're making really large batches, you will want to use standard baking sheets.

It can be difficult to fit that many iron skillets into your oven.

Cherry Chews

The dried cherries are so sweet that you won't need much sugar in this recipe at all. But if you like your cookies really sweet, you might want to add an extra ¼ cup turbinado sugar.

4 tablespoons butter
4 tablespoons Neufchatel cheese
¼ cup turbinado sugar
¾ cup banana, fine dice
½ cup dried black cherries, snipped into quarters
and soaked in
½ cup rum
1 cup flour
powdered sugar
24 whole dried black cherries (not soaked)

Cream butter, add Neufchatel cheese and cream together, beat in sugar until well mixed.

Stir in diced banana. Drain soaked dried cherries, reserving rum for another use. Stir in cherries; stir to blend well. Stir in flour and beat resulting sticky, stiff batter thoroughly until no pockets of flour remain on bottom or sides of bowl.

Dust palms with powdered sugar. By the tablespoon, roll batter between dusted palms to make balls. Place 1" apart on slightly greased, large cast iron skillet. Push a dried cherry (unsoaked) well into the top of each ball.

Bake in preheated 350-degree oven 20–22 minutes, until bottoms are browned. Remove skillet from oven, and with a spatula remove cookies to a rack to cool. Makes 24.

Chocolate Mint Surprise

The surprise ingredient here is jicama, which lends a crunch without skewing the peppermint flavor, as nuts might. These make a lovely accent to your cookie jar, though they're a little intense to eat all day long. As a dessert they make a nice accompaniment to vanilla flavored frozen yogurt or ice cream.

¾ cup jicama, minced
crème de menthe to cover jicama, about ½ cup
1 stick butter
4 tablespoons olive oil
½ cup turbinado sugar
¼ cup Dutch baker's chocolate (cocoa)
2 teaspoons peppermint extract
1 cup unbleached all-purpose flour

Place minced jicama in a tall, narrow mug. Pour over the jicama enough crème de menthe to cover. Set aside for at least an hour, to give the jicama time to absorb the color and the flavor of the liqueur. Drain; reserve liqueur.

Cream butter, then beat in olive oil a little at a time. Add sugar and cocoa, beating thoroughly after each addition. Add 1 tablespoon of the reserved crème de menthe. Add peppermint extract; beat to blend. Now add drained jicama and mix well.

Stir in flour and mix thoroughly, allowing no flour to remain on bottom or sides of bowl.

Take up by tablespoons, rolling between palms to form balls. Place balls on ungreased cast iron skillet (or standard cookie sheet), leaving an inch on all sides. Flatten with the floured and sugared bottom (to prevent sticking) of a tumbler bearing an interesting pattern.

Bake in preheated 350-degree oven for 18 minutes. Remove skillet from oven and let cookies cool in skillet for 15 minutes before removing to rack for final cooling.

Makes 24.

A Cookie Challenge

Surely by now you've noticed a similarity among most of these cookies: Basically, nine of them are butter cookies rolled between your palms to form a ball, then flattened with a tumbler bottom and imprinted with a decorative pattern. Two of the nine are "thumbprint" cookies that merely substitute your thumb for the tumbler.

This type of cookie is particularly kid-friendly. It's also particularly easy for you—and your youngsters—to customize, once you've caught the hang of it, with your own departures from the flavorings I've used.

Observe the formula:

1. Cream shortening, which can combine butter with olive oil, cream cheese (or Neufchatel cheese), or light sour cream, both to cut calories and to provide a distinctive flavor edge.

2. Beat in sugar, either brown or turbinado.

3. Add flavorings. (Taste the developing product at this point.)

4. If you're using dried fruit, soak it first to add moisture. Soaking in spirits adds extra flavor and gives you a jump-start on another dessert.

5. Add flour (a little at a time, measuring as you go, and striving for the consistency you will have observed in these cookies).

6. Add chopped nuts of some kind, for that satisfying cookie crunch.

7. Roll between palms and make imprints.

8. Bake in preheated 350-degree oven. You must watch your original product closely to determine when it should come out of the oven. Begin checking when the aromas permeate your kitchen—this means the ingredients are volatizing. When your whole house starts smelling like cookies, they're close to being done.

*E*ven meat-and-potato people need a little something on their plates beside the beef or chicken.

In addition to filling up the belly, a carefully chosen starch or vegetable
can extend, point up, ameliorate, or sustain the flavor of the entrée.
For instance, the brisk crispness of **Chayote Squash and Fennel**
makes a fine counterpoint to the dusky **Savory Tender Goat**.

The right starch can cradle or soak up a delicious sauce
as adroitly as mashed potatoes cosset a fine gravy.
Wild Rice Casserole is delightfully graced by the port wine reduction sauce of **Lamb and Bamb**.

Some starches prepared for dinner can hold over as the foundation for a fine breakfast.
Consider how **Creekside** builds upon **Cabin Fried Potatoes.**

And some dishes start out with beans or peas and just grow from there,
as **New Year's Peas** tends to morph into a full-fledged lunch dish.

So here's our tribute to the magical vegetable kingdom.
Root, leaf, seed, and stem, we thank you.

Cabin Fried Potatoes

This dish works well alone, as a side dish, or as a basis for **Creekside** *(page 12).*

2 large potatoes (about 1 pound), any variety, chopped medium dice
2 medium onions, any variety, chopped small dice
1 cup baby sweet peppers, chopped small dice (optional)
3 tablespoons meat fat (bacon drippings, beef, or chicken fat [see pages 68 & 72])
   if you don't have meat fat, use canola oil
1 tablespoon paprika
salt and pepper to taste
parsley, dried or fresh (optional)
light sour cream (optional)
chives (optional)

In a large (10- to 12-inch) cast iron skillet, heat the fat until almost smoking. Throw in the potatoes, sprinkle with salt and pepper, and sauté, using spatula to turn constantly. Adjust heat so the potatoes don't burn.

This will take about 10 to 15 minutes of attention.

When potatoes yield easily to a fork, throw in the onions and peppers, sprinkle the paprika over, and continue to sauté, stirring. Adjust heat as necessary; continue to stir. Don't let anything burn. When onions are translucent, your dish is done. You can garnish this dish with chopped parsley, dried or fresh, and/or sour cream or chives.

This will hold (uncovered) in a warm oven or on a very low back burner, until you prepare any main dish you wish to serve it with. This dish goes very well with a number of other entrées, and is the basis for Creekside. Serves 2 generously as a side dish (with some left over for the wife's lunch or for the dog), or can easily be increased to serve as many as you want.

Parsley Potatoes

Yukon Golds work well in this recipe.

4 medium-sized potatoes, scrubbed and cut into large chunks
1 tablespoon butter
2 tablespoons parsley, dried or fresh (chopped)
salt and pepper to taste

In a 2-quart saucepan—I use an enameled saucepan for this recipe, though it's not really necessary—bring the potatoes to a boil in water to just barely cover. Cut heat back to a medium simmer. Cook, covered, until potatoes are firm to the fork but not hard, maybe 10 minutes. Don't let them get mushy.

Drain the water (you might want to save this potato water for use in baking **City Bread** (page 126). Throw in butter and parsley. Holding the lid on the pan, shake vigorously to coat potatoes with butter and parsley. Salt and pepper to taste. Serves 4.

Variations:

Add Italian seasoning along with the parsley. Add a little onions and garlic sautéed in a little olive oil.

Parsnip Mashed Potatoes

If this dish isn't on our Thanksgiving table, Matt is in trouble. Even though it doesn't use cast iron, its distinctive flavor earns it a spot in this book. You'll be glad.

10 medium-sized Yukon Gold potatoes, peeled and cut in 1" chunks
2 medium-sized parsnips, peeled and cut in 1" chunks
8 tablespoons butter, melted
¾ cup milk or cream, warmed
½ teaspoon salt

Boil the potatoes and parsnips in water to barely cover. Cook until just fork-tender but not mushy.

Drain potatoes and parsnips, put in the bowl of your Kitchen-Aid, and use the wire whisk to whip the potatoes. Slowly add warm milk and melted butter. You don't have to use all the butter or all the milk. Stop adding when you like the consistency of the potatoes. If you don't have or don't want to use your Kitchen-Aid, use a ricer. This works just as well. It's a little more work, but then again, you don't have to clean the Kitchen-Aid.

Turn mashed potatoes into a *heated* ceramic serving bowl. Mashed potatoes like to be served immediately; however, if there is an unavoidable delay, set the mashed potatoes over almost simmering water. (You can use the water they were boiled in.) Save the potato water to add to your bread recipes or to any stock you may be building.

For garnish I like to throw a little paprika on top, maybe a pat of butter in the middle, and some chives or parsley around the edges. Serves 8, or 6 with leftovers for fried potato patties in the morning.

Polenta Pie

This is obviously not a low-cal dish. Use sparingly.

1 cup polenta
4 cups water
1 teaspoon salt
1 tablespoon butter
½ cup grated Asiago cheese
½ cup Gorgonzola cheese

In a medium-sized saucepan, add salt to water; bring to a boil. Gradually add polenta to boiling salted water, stirring constantly until thickened. This will take about 15 to 20 minutes of constant attention. If you have to leave for any reason, get somebody to keep stirring the pan. When polenta is thick, add butter and cheese. Mix well.

Melt 1 tablespoon of chicken fat in a #8 cast iron skillet, swirling to coat the sides. Pour polenta into the greased skillet. Sprinkle Gorgonzola evenly over the top.

Bake 25 minutes in a 350-degree oven or until Gorgonzola is bubbling. Remove from oven, place on cooling rack, and allow to rest for a few minutes. Serve warm in skillet or you can let this completely cool and serve sliced.

Serves 6 to 8 as a side dish.

Oven-Roasted Vegetables

The trick to this dish is to get the vegetables somewhat crisp but not burnt. Jicama is a surprise ingredient here: its crispy sweetness will delight your guests.

olive oil
2 medium potatoes, unpeeled but scrubbed,
   chopped into large cubes
2 medium onions, peeled and cut into chunks
1 large jicama, peeled and chopped into large cubes
3 large carrots, unpeeled,
   cut diagonally into slices about ½ inch thick
1 large parsnip, peeled and cut into chunks
1 each sweet red and yellow peppers,
   cut into large chunks
12 garlic cloves, peeled
salt and pepper
Italian seasoning (optional)

Drizzle 2 tablespoons olive oil onto large rimmed baking sheet. Depending on how many vegetables, you may need two baking sheets.

Toss cut vegetables together with 1 tablespoon or so of olive oil, to coat. Spread vegetables in a single layer on rimmed baking pans; don't crowd them.

Drizzle more olive oil over vegetables, salt and pepper to taste, and sprinkle with Italian seasoning (optional).

Put in preheated 450-degree oven. After 10 minutes, remove from oven and stir to rearrange. Restore to oven for approximately another 10 to 15 minutes. Keep a close eye on them so they don't burn.

Remove from oven, place in warm serving bowl, turn oven off. Serve immediately or hold in warm oven until ready to serve.

If at this point you want to take the time and trouble, you can deglaze the baking pans with water that you then pour into any stock you may have going. Deglazing the pans at this point will make them a lot easier to clean.

Serves 6.

Makes a great accompaniment for pot roast, short ribs, chicken, or any roasted or braised meat. Leftovers can be combined with any leftover meat to make an excellent breakfast hash.

This recipe can easily be reduced to make 2 or 3 servings and can be cooked in your large cast iron skillet.

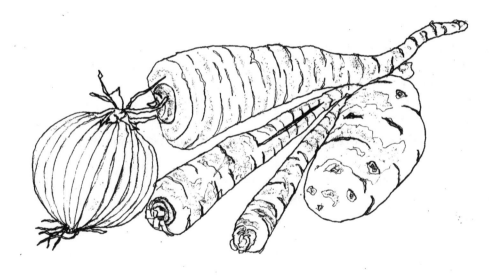

Wild Rice Casserole

Here's another dish you can do ahead, the day before, and pop in the oven to warm before serving. This is an excellent accompaniment for lamb dishes. The leftovers are great.

1 cup wild rice (the pure thing, not a mix)
2 cups boiling water
½ cup slivered almonds
½ cup dried mushrooms, reconstituted in warm
  water to cover
¼ cup sundried tomatoes, chopped
¼ cup dry sherry or port
1 tablespoon butter
dried or fresh parsley, chopped, to garnish

Put wild rice in a 2-quart saucepan and pour boiling water over it. Let sit for 3 to 4 hours. Bring back to a boil, cover, and reduce to a low simmer. Cook 90 minutes or until water is fully absorbed.

Turn into a greased, high-sided, 2-quart ovenproof serving dish. Add slivered almonds, mushrooms, and dried tomatoes. Add sherry or, if you're feeling extravagant, ¼ cup of your best port.

Mix well, cover, and bake in preheated 350-degree oven for 30 minutes. Uncover, and bake for another 10 minutes. Remove from oven. Mix in butter. Fluff with fork. Garnish with parsley, either dried or chopped fresh.

Serves 6 as a side dish.

Variations:

You can use this same recipe with a mixture of rices: half brown rice, half wild rice is good, or come up with your own combination of rices.

New Year's Peas

With mustard greens and corn bread on the side, this dish makes a complete, hearty meal.

1¾ cups dried black-eyed peas
3 quarts cold water
2 smoked ham hocks, 2½ to 3 pounds total weight
1 tablespoon olive oil
1 medium onion, finely diced
¾ cup celery, finely sliced
1 tablespoon fennel seed

In a large saucepan, add peas to cold water. Bring to boil, reduce to simmer, and cook until *al dente*, about 45 minutes. When peas are cooked, strain and reserve liquid for use in stocks or soups. Turn peas into ovenproof serving dish.

While peas are cooking, place hocks on a rack in a #8 cast iron skillet. Roast hocks in preheated 350 degree oven for 30 minutes. When hocks are cooked, remove from oven and cut meat off bones, discarding fat and gristle (or save for dog snacks). Cut meat into large dice and add to peas.

Deglaze the roasting pan with water. Add olive oil, onion, celery, and fennel seed and sauté briefly. Add to peas and meat. Toss to mix. Serves 4.

Accompaniments:

Serve with **Corn Bread** (page 132) and steamed chard or mustard greens.

Variations:

Instead of smoked ham hocks, you can use ¼ pound of salt pork. Cut in small dice, parboil to leach out excess salt, then try out in cast iron skillet. Add to peas in the same manner as you would the ham hocks (described above).

Savory Adzuki Beans

Amazingly savory for a vegetarian bean recipe. This dish requires those ancient little red adzuki beans; none others will do.

2 quarts salted pasta water (as much as you have left over after cooking half a pound of pasta)
½ pound adzuki beans
½ cup sweet red pepper, sliced and diced,
or 4 or 5 baby sweet peppers, sliced
½ cup onions, sliced and diced
2 cloves garlic, peeled, crushed, and diced
2 tablespoons olive oil
cilantro to garnish (optional)

Suppose you have leftover pasta water (which you should have, after having cooked pasta: I never throw it out). Throw in half a pound of adzuki beans and let them sit overnight in the same large saucepan you cooked the pasta in in the first place. About an hour before you want to eat the beans, set them to boiling in that same large saucepan, then reduce the heat to a low simmer and continue to cook.

Meanwhile, slice and dice some baby sweet peppers (green, red, yellow), an onion, and a couple of cloves of garlic. In a #8 cast iron skillet, saute in 2 tablespoons olive oil over high heat until limp. Throw these in the large saucepan with the beans and continue to cook until beans are tender, about an hour or so.

When beans are tender, strain, reserving liquid, and place in a serving dish (ceramic bean pot, whatever). Take about 4 or 5 tablespoons of the beans out of the serving dish and put them in the skillet in which you sautéed the vegetables, along with some of the reserved bean liquid. Mash the beans in the skillet. Thicken by boiling the mixture down.

Pour the thickened, mashed bean mixture back over the beans in the serving pot. Garnish with cilantro or whatever and serve. Add no extra salt; the salt in the pasta water will be enough.

Serves 4–6.

Baked Beans

As with chili and many other things, there are a lot of recipes for baked beans. If you're in a hurry you can pick up a few cans in the store and doctor 'em up a bit, but they won't be anywhere near this recipe.

1 pound dry navy beans
4 quarts water
2 pounds smoked ham hocks
6 cloves garlic, crushed, peeled, and diced small
1 or 2 baby green or red or yellow peppers, diced (optional)
1 medium onion, cut medium dice
2 tablespoons brown sugar or maple syrup
1 tablespoon white vinegar
½ teaspoon dry mustard
¼ teaspoon salt
¼ teaspoon black pepper

Boil the dry beans in water until just barely *al dente.* This is important; you don't want mush here. This will take an hour or so, maybe longer, depending on the age and tenderness of the beans. Strain, reserving liquid.

While beans are cooking, parboil ham hocks in water to cover. Pull the ham hocks out after 45 minutes or so. Discard the water. Put ham hocks back in the pot they just came out of; cover with cold water. Cut off all skin and visible fat from ham hocks. Dice meat medium dice.

Mix together all remaining ingredients: garlic, peppers, onion, brown sugar or maple syrup, vinegar, mustard, salt, and pepper. Throw it all into the bean pot. Pour reserved bean liquid over to just barely cover.

Place, covered, in 300° oven for 3 to 4 hours. Check every hour, adding liquid if necessary. Remove cover for last half hour. Serve immediately, or keep warm until ready to serve. Serves 4 for dinner.

Serve with **Skillet Cornbread**.

This recipe can easily be ramped up for a crowd. Just use 4–5 pounds of beans and increase proportions on everything else. Throw it in your big bean pot and put it in the pit with the pig.

Chayote Squash and Fennel

If you've never met this vegetable before, this squash that looks like a hard, green pear, it's worth seeking out for its crunch and briskness. This pristine cooking method lets its nutty, slightly sweet flavor shine through. The fennel bulb is a perfect flavor partner. Try it once and you'll come back for more, for sure.

2 Chayote squashes
2 tablespoons bulb of fresh fennel, cut small dice
2-3 tablespoons olive oil
salt and pepper to taste

Cut squash in ½-inch chunks and fennel in small dice. Heat olive oil in skillet. Sauté briefly and vigorously until squash is fork-tender but not mushy. Turn off heat, cover skillet, let rest for a few minutes to absorb the oils, then serve. Serves 4 as a side dish.

Variations:

I like to add a few splashes of white vinegar while the skillet is on the heat and toss in air. This gives a nice flambé and also adds a nice flavor. Immediately turn off the heat and cover.

Green Beans in Olive Oil

1 pound fresh young green beans
2 tablespoons olive oil
½ cup slivered almonds
1 tablespoon white wine vinegar

String the beans and slice diagonally in 2- to 3-inch pieces. In a cast iron skillet, heat 2 tablespoons olive oil until almost smoking. Throw in the beans and sauté quickly. Since these are fresh beans, you really don't need to cook them any length of time; just heat them thoroughly and coat with olive oil. Keep the pan moving so they don't burn.

Throw in half a cup of slivered almonds and sauté for another 30 seconds or so over medium-high heat. Throw in a tablespoon of white wine vinegar. This will cause an impressive flambé. Turn off the heat. Either serve immediately or keep warm until serving. Serves 4.

Variations:

Add Italian seasoning or any compatible herbs or spices.

Chilled Garbanzos and Anchovies

This recipe benefits greatly from an overnight rest in the refrigerator. Leftovers keep very well in the refrigerator (covered) for up to a week.

2 cans garbanzo beans, drained
½ cup fresh parsley, chopped fine
2 tablespoons olive oil
1 tablespoon red wine vinegar
1 hard-boiled egg, chopped medium dice
4 anchovy filets, chopped medium
1 tablespoon capers, drained (optional)
1 teaspoon fresh cilantro, chopped fine
1 medium red onion, chopped fine dice

Mix all ingredients in a large bowl and toss. Chill 1 hour in refrigerator and serve on cold plates.
Serves 6 as a side dish.

Spinach and Calamari

This dish can be served either hot or cold. The secret to this dish is to not overcook the calamari. If it is cooked too long, it will toughen, and then your only alternative is to add water and/or white wine, then poach for at least 20 minutes and serve over pasta.

4 medium whole calamari, about 1 pound, cleaned and cut into 1" rings
3–4 tablespoons olive oil
1 medium onion, chopped small dice
6 cloves garlic, crushed, peeled, and chopped small dice
½ pound fresh spinach, cleaned and coarsely chopped
1 tablespoon red wine vinegar
¼ cup feta cheese, crumbled

Pat calamari dry. Heat olive oil in cast iron skillet until almost smoking. Throw in one-half the chopped onions and one-half the garlic. Add the calamari. Sauté briefly—and I do mean *briefly*—over medium heat, no more than 2 minutes. Set your timer.

Put chopped and drained spinach in a salad bowl. Pour contents of skillet over spinach. Add remaining onions and garlic. Add red wine vinegar. Toss, arrange on salad plates, then sprinkle feta cheese over. Serve immediately or chill in refrigerator. Serves 2.

Serve with cruets of olive oil and vinegar.

Variations:

This dish can also be served as a chilled salad.

Steamed Artichokes

Artichokes ("chokes") are endemic to California. Those who have never seen them would say "cactus." They are not actually cactus, but thistles, and ugly as they appear, are delightful when cooked.

4 artichokes
water to bring up to one-quarter height of
   artichokes
¼ cup olive oil
1 cup white wine
⅛ teaspoon lemon pepper

Cut off stems and spiny points of each leaf. Open artichoke. Remove inner small leaves and fibrous material on top of the artichoke heart. Place upright in a kettle.

Whip together the olive oil, wine, and lemon pepper. Pour into the artichokes. Steam, covered, about 45 minutes or until tender, checking occasionally and adding more water if necessary. Serve hot on salad plates. Serves 4.

Variations:

Put ½ teaspoon pungent cheese—such as Gorgonzola, bleu, Stilton, or whatever—into the heart of each artichoke.

Easy Cauliflower Slightly Mejicana

Colorful as well as flavorful, this dish brings a touch of fiesta to your table. Don't throw away the leftover nopalitos and tomatoes. Use them to combine with browned ground beef and some **Garlic Black Beans** *for a quick, tasty, mild chili.*

½ **medium onion, chopped small dice**
1 **clove garlic, crushed and diced**
1 **tablespoon olive oil**
1 **cup Mexican-style tomatoes with chiles**
¼ **cup canned nopalitos (cactus)**
1 **large head cauliflower with all its leaves**

In a #8 cast iron skillet (for which you have a lid), over medium heat, sauté onion and garlic in olive oil until onion is translucent. Add canned Mexican-style tomatoes (along with can juices) and canned nopalitos. Stir to blend.

Cut cauliflower florets away from head and set aside. Trim cauliflower leaves away from head, preserving as much of the green material as possible. Line a serving bowl with these leaves. You are creating a green nest in which to present the cauliflower and tomatoes.

Add florets to skillet with the tomatoes and nopalitos. Cover the skillet and steam vegetables over medium-high heat until cauliflower is fork-tender but not all limp and soggy.

Remove vegetables, place in cauliflower nest, and turn up heat under the juices remaining in the skillet. Cook, stirring, until juices are reduced to about ¼ cup. Pour over cauliflower. Serve hot. Serves 4.

Stone---

Yesterday I started one or two of my three annual large-scale stock-making operations. Last year I had gone to the slaughterhouse and bought fifty pounds of beef bones for ten dollars. I used half of them last year and I'm using the remaining twenty-five pounds this year.

I defrosted the twenty-five frozen pounds, put them on large baking pans (12 x 18), sprinkled salt and pepper over them, and put them in a 400 degree oven for about an hour or so. Turned the heat off, left them in the oven overnight.

This morning I threw them in a large (25 quart) spigoted (which is very nice, for it simplifies things greatly) stockpot that Linda gave me for Christmas year before last. I then scraped the grease off the pans and threw that also in the stockpot.

I used a pound each of celery, carrots, and onions, and I would recommend a pound of leeks, but I was too cheap to pay $3.98 a pound for them. I distributed those on the baking pans, drizzled olive oil over them, salted and peppered them, put them in the oven (350) for about an hour or so. When they came out I dumped them in the stockpot.

I then deglazed the pans with cold water and poured the liquid into the stockpot, also throwing in a handful of peppercorns, three fresh bay leaves, some dried thyme and dried tarragon, and about a dozen whole cloves. Then I poured into the stockpot about two more quarts of *cold* water. Turned the heat up high under the stockpot. I then went to the refrigerator and pulled out all the ice the icemaker had made and dumped it into the stockpot. The idea here is to bring the liquid level up to about three-quarters of the height of the solid ingredients. (Whenever adding water to a stock, use either very cold water or ice. This will help the stock to fall clear. Never add hot or warm water.)

When the ice had melted, I brought the uncovered pot back to a boil, and immediately cut it down to a very slow simmer, just barely ticking. I stirred it every once in a while and, depending on how it smells and looks, I might leave it on a very low simmer, uncovered, all night—I haven't decided yet.

* * * * *

I did leave the stock on the stove at a very, very low simmer all night. We awoke to beautiful aromas.

I took the large pot off the stove, opened the spigot, and drained the liquid into another large spigoted (11-quart) stockpot, straining it through a medium sieve. This pot I covered (since it was raining) and set outside to cool. Later today, around 3 p.m., I brought it in. It had formed a half-inch cap of fat.

I opened the spigot of the 11-quart stockpot and ran the liquid through a fine chinois. I then remelted the fat and saved back a small amount, which I will freeze and use very sparingly as flavoring in hash browns, when browning chicken or other meats, and many other purposes I can't think of now, including dog food. It provides a great flavor edge to other dishes, but I don't care what your Healthy Cook says; this fat has NO PLACE in a fine stock or sauce: it will RUIN it.

I put the stock back on the stove, where I am again simmering it very slowly, skimming off what little scum seems to be arising. This stock fell amazingly clear, so I think we should have a good one here. I haven't yet decided how far I'm going to reduce it.

I gave Bucky one of the large bones today. He took it out in the back yard and ate the whole thing. I also gave him some of the detritus mixed with his kibbles. He's a lucky dog.

I further reduced the stock by about one-quarter, then drained it again out of the spigot through the chinois into a tall stainless steel pot. This pot does not have a spigot. Back on the stove at a very low simmer and reduced this again by about a quarter.

I then took about three quarts out of this pot, putting it in another, smaller (6½ quart), stainless steel pot. The remaining liquid constitutes "the stock."

The liquid that I took out, I reduced again by half, which made it into a syrupy glace. Today I have to go out and buy some ice cube trays. I will then pour the glace into the ice-cube trays, freeze, then pop the cubes out and put them in Zip-loc bags back in the freezer. I call these my "beef bullets." They have concentrated and intense flavor. I use these in dishes for the two of us, such as a bernaise sauce over steak or lamb chops*, or I'll toss one or two into my Grizzy #8 when making a Chicken Marsala.

The stock I pour into 8- to 10-ounce plastic containers, mark them, and put them in the freezer. This stock is used for pot roast, short ribs of beef, goat stew, and a lot of other things I can't think of right now.

So, starting out with 25 pounds of bones and 5 to 6 pounds of vegetables and almost 5 gallons of water, we end up with maybe a gallon and a half of stock and a couple dozen beef bullets. And a week's work.

*[Steve, it is worth every minute of his time, in terms of effect of the finished dish. His lamb chops with a beef bullet bernaise sauce had me rolling my eyes in ecstasy when we were courting.]

Good luck on building your stock.

Matt

Stock-making is a worthy endeavor, best undertaken in the winter when the forecast is for rain or snow over the next four or five days. All of this can be done in much smaller quantities using the same method. Any of the recipes in this book that call for stock can use as a substitute the canned varieties available from your supermarket, but the flavors *will not be the same.*

A spigoted container is not necessary—indeed, it is expensive and hard to come by—but for the cook who truly enjoys making stock and does it regularly (at least once or twice a year), such an extravagance is worth it, for it makes it easier. (See page 163 for an online supplier.)

Any red meat will serve as the basis for your stock. The carcass of a deer, when chopped, makes an excellent base for a venison stock, in addition to honoring the animal by using all its parts. It is important to either chop or saw the large bones so that the marrow flavor gets into the stock.

Chicken Stock

Chicken stock is not as labor-intensive as beef stock. It uses the same ingredients, substituting only chicken carcasses for beef bones.

Sometimes I will buy two or more whole chickens on sale. I usually cook one of them whole that evening (see **Birds in Iron,** page 94); the other(s) I dissect into pieces, boning out the breast. I then vacuum seal and freeze the chicken pieces in meal-sized packages for two.

Now, as to the remaining carcasses: I chop them with a meat cleaver, throw the pieces of bones into a plastic bag, and freeze. When I've accumulated 5 to 6 pounds of chicken detritus, I thaw them out and follow the beef stock recipe (see pages 63–65) up to the point of reducing the stock.

For chicken stock, after it is strained and defatted I usually only reduce it a little—maybe one-quarter. Then I freeze it in 2-cup (16 ounce) containers.

In a pinch, chicken stock can be further reduced and substituted for beef stock. I also use it as a base for most soups.

Quick Chicken or Turkey Stock

After you've roasted and served a full bird (see **Birds in Iron** page 94), take the carcass and the leftover bones and chop them with a meat cleaver, large dice.

In a large Dutch oven, throw in 1 cup sliced and diced celery, 2 medium carrots large dice, 2 medium onions cut large dice, 8 cloves of crushed garlic, 2 tablespoons canola oil. Saute briefly over high heat.

Throw in bones and 1 bay leaf. Pour in cold water up to three-quarters the height of the contents of Dutch oven. Bring to a rolling boil. Reduce to a low simmer. Let simmer 3 to 4 hours, adding cold water or ice if necessary to keep the liquid level between half and three-quarters the height of contents.

Strain and degrease. You now have stock.

As we mentioned in the Introduction, some of these recipes require four days from start to finish, but let that not dissuade you: no meat recipe requires more than one hour of total hands-on time.

All meat recipes that require long preparation times *can* be made more quickly, but there will be some significant loss of flavor. You *can* go to the supermarket, buy a cut of beef, and make, the very same day, a pot roast that will satisfy and nourish your family and guests. But it will not bear the inimitably dusky, intensely carnal flavor of the pot roast made from aged beef, the one we designate as Noble Pot Roast.

These days we've been enjoying grass-fed beef and experimenting with goat, that low-cholesterol, high-flavor, biblical meat. The goat in particular benefits from long, slow cooking, but if you have no Dutch oven, do not despair: your countertop slow cooker will take over where your skillet leaves off.

Still, there are times, at the end of a hectic day, when life's urgencies demand that you put together a meal *right now*. Be not dismayed: these pages contain many a recipe to swiftly satisfy your hungry crew.

After all, one of us has been a single father, a sailor, and a mountain man. He knows from many years of experience how to whip up a tasty meal in a hurry.

Noble Pot Roast or Short Ribs of Beef

Allow 4 to 5 days from start to finish. Please read discussion at least twice before beginning recipe.

Followed to the letter, this recipe produces a noble dish. We've seen guests roll their eyes and come back for seconds, thirds, and, yes, even fourths. Made with substitutions, it will still be good, but not great.

Don't be put off by all the dialog: Though this dish sounds complicated, it's really simple and easy to make. Please read the following discussion at least twice before attempting this recipe.

This recipe can be used for either cut of meat—pot roast or short ribs--the method is exactly the same. We have served both variations to family and friends many times, to unanimously high acclaim (except for a "yuck" from one 4-year-old granddaughter, who only eats noodles).

The recipe can be varied many ways, but there are three essential ingredients without which you will still have a fine pot roast, but nowhere near the excellence of which this dish is capable. The three ingredients are aged beef, your good stock (see page 68), and meat fat that you have saved in the freezer (can be beef, chicken, venison, bear, whatever).

Although production time is long, hands-on preparation time is less than an hour. This recipe is great for company because it can be prepared well ahead of time and slammed into the oven a few hours before your guests arrive. All that will be required is to pull it out, garnish it, and set it on the table.

The basic secret of this recipe is well-aged beef. I will buy a pot roast or short ribs when I see them on sale because they are nearing or are at the pull date.

(Consider buying two or more and ageing them as follows, then vacuum sealing and freezing those you're not going to use immediately. This gives you aged meat ready to go in one day rather than four or five.)

At home I take the meat out of the package, put it on a rack over a cooking sheet or baking pan, salt and pepper all sides, cover lightly with a paper towel, and put it in the refrigerator (a top shelf is preferable).

Leave the meat in the refrigerator for at least four days, turning once a day. On the fifth day, or when you intend to cook the meat, bring it out of the refrigerator. It will have lost perhaps five percent of its weight and will look dark, not red. (At this point your wife may make you throw it away because it looks "spoiled.") Dust meat *lightly* with flour.

Heat 2 to 3 tablespoons of any meat or chicken fat to almost smoking in a large cast-iron Dutch oven on top of the stove. Brown the meat on all sides. If the pot roast is too big to fit, cut it and brown in pieces, though it is better to use a large enough pan to brown it all at once.

Remove from Dutch oven and drain on paper towels. Pour off excess fat, if any. Deglaze the pot with a dry red wine, then turn heat off, leaving any deglazing liquid in the pot. Put meat back in Dutch oven. Add enough stock (page 68) to cover all but the top quarter of the meat. Bring to a boil, uncovered, on top of stove. Reduce to very low simmer.

Now, there are three ways to cook this dish from this point on: on top of the stove, in the oven (which is probably the best), or on top of your wood stove at the cabin (my preferred method).

If cooking on top of the stove, either range or wood stove, cover with the tight-fitting Dutch oven lid and continue at a very low simmer. (If the lid is not tight-fitting, seal with aluminum foil.)

If cooking in the oven, preheat to 450°, put the tightly covered Dutch oven into oven, turn heat down to 325°, and close the oven door.

Depending on the quality and quantity of meat, it will probably take anywhere from two to four hours to cook from this point on, whether on top of the stove or in the oven. Check the meat after an hour, adding more stock if necessary, then check every half hour after that, adding stock if necessary. Meat is done when tender to the fork but not falling off the bone. You want this meat to have some "tooth" when it is finally served.

Remove pot from heat, set on cooling rack, let cool for 15 to 20 minutes. Pluck out the meat, set aside on a dish, strain liquid through a coarse strainer, and, if you want to be real fancy, run it through a chinois. Put strained liquid into a gravy grease separator, letting any residual fat rise to the top. Return meat to the Dutch oven and put the lid back on.

Allow both containers (the Dutch oven containing the meat and the gravy grease separator containing the strained liquid) to cool, then put both containers and their contents into the refrigerator overnight.

At this juncture the dish is essentially finished.

Approximately three hours before serving, bring both containers out of the refrigerator. Skim the congealed fat off the liquid or pour out liquid from the bottom spout. (You might want to save this fat because it has tremendous flavor for hash-browns, onions, or your next pot roast.)

Pour skimmed liquid into the Dutch oven containing the meat. Put the covered Dutch oven into a preheated 300-degree oven. After an hour or so the dish is in a holding pattern and can be served at any time. That's what makes it so nice for company.

Variations to this recipe can include adding reconstituted dried mushrooms and/or sundried tomatoes before the final heating. Also Italian or other seasoning, whichever direction you want to take it. It should be emphasized, however, that this is a very good dish without any further machinations.

Leftovers can be vacuum sealed and frozen to provide a very satisfying meal when time is short.

Accompaniments can include **Parsnip Mashed Potatoes** (page 54), **Parsley Potatoes** (page 53), or **Oven Roasted Vegetables** (page 56).

Wine suggestion: a full-bodied red of not great expense, a rustic wine that will pair well with the earthy flavors of this dish.

You just have to taste this dish to believe it, and having tasted it, we guarantee the flavor will linger in your memory.

Ingredients

4 to 5 pounds beef
   7-bone chuck roast is best,
   but other cuts will work
If using short ribs,
   have butcher cut into 2- to 3-inch lengths
meat fat: beef, chicken, or venison
   (canola oil will work, but you'll lose some flavor)
1 quart of your good homemade stock
   (you probably won't use this much,
   but you can refreeze whatever is left)
If you *must*, substitute low-sodium beef or chicken
   broth, but be aware that you have lost an
   important essence
salt and pepper
flour
1 cup dry red wine

Method Summary (please read discussion before beginning this recipe)

Heat meat fat and brown aged beef in large Dutch oven. Remove and drain browned meat; pour off excess fat, if any, from Dutch oven. Deglaze pot with wine, turn off heat. Put meat back in pot. Add stock, bring to boil (uncovered), reduce to simmer. Cook, covered, on top of stove or in 325-degree oven. Check occasionally; add more stock if necessary. When meat yields easily to a fork, remove from heat and let cool 15-20 minutes. Strain and degrease liquid, then refrigerate liquid and meat (in their separate containers) overnight. Three hours before serving, skim congealed fat off liquid and return to Dutch oven containing the meat. Hold all in a 300-degree oven for at least an hour or until ready to serve. Serves 6 to 8.

Braised Oxtail

This is an adaptation of a recipe sent from Brazil by my friend Harry. They use a large pressure cooker for this dish. We don't have a pressure cooker, but it works very well in the Dutch oven.

Buy a lot of oxtails. There isn't much meat on them, and everyone eats a lot because this dish is very good. Around here, oxtails are usually over three dollars a pound, which is a lot when you consider that there's not much meat on them. However, we discovered that the local slaughterhouse sells them eight pounds for ten dollars, which is more than reasonable.

8 pounds oxtail
salt and pepper
2–3 tablespoons canola oil
1–2 cups Marsala or other semisweet red wine
2 cups beef stock (page 68)
  or chicken stock (page 70)
1 cup fresh parsley or cilantro, chopped,
  OR ½ cup dried

Remove excess fat from oxtails. (Fried into cracklings, this makes excellent doggie snacks.) Salt and pepper oxtails on all sides. Place oxtails on racks over cookie sheets. Put paper towel over; place in refrigerator for 3 to 5 days. Turn once a day.

When ready to begin cooking, add canola oil to your largest skillet. Brown the meat on all sides, in batches. As they are browned, put pieces in large cast iron Dutch oven.

Deglaze the large skillet with Marsala or other semisweet red wine. Scrape with spatula to loosen fond. Pour deglazing liquid and fond over the tails. Add 2 cups of your good stock (or more if you can spare it). Add enough water or wine to bring liquid up to just over half the height of the meat.

Bring to boil, reduce to low simmer, and cover. At this point you have three choices: You can continue to simmer on your kitchen range, you can move the Dutch oven to your wood stove, or you can cook it in your oven. If you cook in the oven, preheat to 375 degrees. Put the Dutch oven in, and after 10 minutes turn the heat down to 325 degrees.

The oven method is the most efficient, since it surrounds the Dutch oven with heat, which means the meat is less likely to burn and stick to the bottom.

Oxtails will take anywhere from 2 to 4 hours to cook. After one hour, check; add liquid if necessary to keep liquid level to around half the height of the meat. It may be necessary to adjust heat. You want this to be at a dead-slow simmer. Check again every half hour, adjusting heat and liquids as necessary.

When meat is fork-tender but not falling off the bones, the oxtails are done. Remove Dutch oven from heat. Strain liquid from oxtails into a bowl. Separate fat from the stock using a gravy grease separator or place in the refrigerator until a grease cap forms. Remove grease cap; add what will now be gelatin back to the meat.

Reheat Dutch oven containing oxtails and gelatinous liquid over low heat on stove top, adding chopped parsley or cilantro. You are now in a holding pattern. Either keep warm on stove top over very low heat (you don't want to burn this dish and have things stick to the bottom), or, better yet, put in warm oven until ready to serve.

We usually just serve this in the Dutch oven it was cooked in—it adds a certain rustic flavor to the table. Serves 6.

Variations:

If you don't have any of your good beef stock, you *can* use your chicken stock. If you have neither of these, store-bought low-sodium beef or chicken stock will work.

Accompaniments:

Mountain Bread (page 130) or **City Bread** (page 126) or **Quick and Easy Garlic Bread** (page 133) or a good store-bought sourdough.

Parsnip Mashed Potatoes (page 54) are good to hold the gravy. **Oven Roasted Vegetables** (page 56) would be good. Also, a lightly dressed fresh green salad.

Wine recommendation:

We like a good high-quality Chianti with this (not the straw basket variety). Or any other robust red wine.

Noble Brisket of Beef

If you can, buy a complete brisket of beef. This will be a large piece of meat—10 to 12 pounds. A full cooked brisket will serve 15 to 20 people. When you buy the brisket, you may want to cut it in half. One half you can cook immediately; the other half you can vacuum seal and freeze for use at a later date. Or you may want to just cook the whole thing and vacuum seal and freeze the leftovers.

Cut off the excess fat, which you will vacuum seal and freeze. (Among other things, this is useful for making **Lucky Dog Treats**, page 156.)

Rub the meat on all sides with your favorite rub. I used to make my rubs from scratch, but there are so many good ones readily available, it's not worth the trouble. Be careful to get one that's not too salty.

Put the rubbed brisket on a rack and place the racked brisket on a rimmed shallow roasting pan or rimmed cookie sheet. Place in the refrigerator, cover lightly with a paper towel, and let age at least 4 days, turning every day.

The morning of the day you're ready to begin cooking, pull the brisket out of the refrigerator and let come to room temperature. Tear off a piece of heavy-duty aluminum foil large enough to enwrap the brisket. Drizzle olive oil on the foil and place thereon a couple of sliced onions; one long carrot, sliced lengthwise; celery stalks cut about 5-6 inches long; maybe a few sweet peppers, sliced, if you have them; and half a dozen crushed garlic cloves.

Place brisket on top of this mirepoix, drizzle a little more olive oil, this time on top of the brisket, and on top of the brisket duplicate the same mirepoix you've just used beneath the meat. Place some of the vegetables alongside the meat. (The idea here is to keep the foil from contacting the meat.)

Now, over this whole mess pour a cup or so of your favorite barbecue sauce. Here again, I used to make my barbecue sauce from scratch, but it's really not worth it because there are so many good ones available off the shelf. I like the thin ones made with a lot of vinegar, but the choice is yours—use whatever you like.

Insert the probe of a meat thermometer into the thickest part of the brisket. Seal the package tightly in the heavy-duty foil—you may need more foil; don't skimp, because you want this package to be tightly sealed.

Place wrapped brisket on rack. Place rack and wrapped brisket on a large cast iron skillet and put everything in a 325-degree oven. Your work is now finished except for keeping a close eye on the thermometer.

Set the thermometer's alarm for 212 degrees. This is the secret to this recipe. I know it sounds like a terribly high temperature to cook any meat to, and right now you're probably thinking, *Tough and dry as an old boot.* Well, not so. The brisket is actually being steamed. By the time it reaches 212 degrees, it will be fork-tender. This will take, depending on the size of the brisket, maybe 4 to 5 hours. Resist the temptation to pull it out before that thermometer hits 212.

When you reach the magic number, pull it out of the oven, take it out of the foil, and set the brisket aside to cool on a rimmed serving platter. You will now have, in the bottom of the foil, a lot of very flavorful juices. Strain juices into a gravy grease separator. Let sit until all grease has risen. The resulting degreased thin stock, mixed with a little barbecue sauce, makes a truly excellent accompaniment for this dish.

Use the now-empty foil as a tent over the brisket as it's cooling. The brisket *must* sit on the cooling platter for at least thirty minutes, during which time it will release and then reabsorb a lot of juice and flavor.

After 30 minutes, slice thin, perpendicular to the grain, and serve with **Mountain Bread**.

An important and tricky variation:

Smoked Brisket

I often prepare this dish at home, then rewrap the brisket lightly in foil and take it and the defatted juices to the ranch, where I finish it in the smoker at a low temperature. I use native oak wood in the smoker, but any local hardwood would work. This gives a delicious smoky flavor to the meat and has our guests clamoring for the recipe. I sometimes "forget" to tell them that it was actually prepared at home and only finished in the smoker, but now you know the whole story.

At the ranch we serve this with corn on the cob, chili beans, **Mountain Bread** (page 130), or **Corn Bread** (page 132). Kegged beer is beverage of choice with this dish. It's a real crowd-pleaser.

Dad's Steak

This is how my father used to barbecue steaks in the back yard when I was a boy.

He would get the charcoal grill glowing red hot and only then would he go to the freezer and select inch-thick Porterhouses or T-bones, which he would throw, solidly frozen, onto the hottest part of the grill.

The fire would roar, splatter, and spit for 3 to 5 minutes before he flipped the steaks to cook for another 3 to 5 minutes.

Then he pulled them off the fire, sprinkled on Roquefort or bleu cheese, which would melt over the steak, and served them on hot plates.

This method produces an excellent rare steak with a nice crust to seal in the juices. Simple, yet quick and effective.

Smoke Alarm Steak or Chops

When you can't get to your outdoor charcoal grill, this is the best way to do it indoors. If your smoke alarm hasn't gone off at least twice during this operation, either you haven't got your skillet hot enough or else you have a truly powerful exhaust fan.

Linda says, "Pure seductive magic for the carnivore. DO use the beef 'bullets' if at ALL possible: they make all the difference between this and ordinary pan-seared steak."

There are two secrets to this recipe: aged meat and beef bullets (page 66). They're worth the time and trouble. Trust us. This recipe is exactly the same whether you use steaks or chops.

1 pound 1" thick New York, Porterhouse, rib eye, filet OR 1 pound 1" thick lamb chops, about ½ pound per serving OR any combination thereof
salt and coarse ground pepper
2 beef bullets
2 teaspoons butter

Sprinkle meat on all sides with salt and coarse ground pepper. Mash into meat with the back of a spoon. Place on rack, place the rack on a plate to catch any blood drippings, lay a paper towel over the meat, and let age in refrigerator for 3 to 5 days.

Remove from refrigerator about 3 to 4 hours before you're ready to fire the dish, to allow meat to arrive at room temperature. Heat a large cast-iron skillet over your hottest burner—you've got to get this really hot—and toss in a dash of salt and a dash of pepper. When skillet begins to smoke, throw in meat. Do not crowd. Sear over high heat 2 minutes—use your timer for this—then flip and sear the other side for 2 timed minutes.

Turn heat down to medium and let cook an additional 2½ minutes on each side for medium rare. Remove meat from skillet, set on warm serving platter, let rest for 5 minutes.

While meat is resting, deglaze the skillet with 2 or more of your good beef bullets (see Stockmaking 101, page 68). Off heat, whisk in 2 teaspoons butter (or more, or less). Pour over meat, serve immediately on warm plates. Serves 2. Double recipe for 4.

Variations:

After the meat comes off the skillet, throw in a cup or so of very thinly sliced onions. Saute until translucent. Place onions over the meat, then deglaze the skillet and continue with the recipe as stated above.

If you don't have beef bullets, deglaze the pan with 1 cup Marsala and reduce it by half. Proceed as above.

Linda's Deer Liver

1 freshly harvested deer liver
salt and pepper
flour
2 tablespoons butter

Process freshly harvested deer liver by soaking in cold water to which you've added a teaspoon of white vinegar. Change water three times, allowing liver to soak a couple of hours in each fresh vinegared water bath.

Pat liver dry. Slice diagonally as thin as possible. Dry slices on paper toweling. Salt and pepper lightly. Dredge in flour on both sides once, then repeat flour dredging on both sides.

Over medium-hot flame, heat butter in cast iron skillet until just sizzling. Quickly sauté floured liver slices, a few at a time. Don't crowd them. When red spots appear in the floured surface facing you, turn liver *only once* and sauté on other side. Each side should take only a minute or so. *Do not overcook.*

Serve immediately, accompanied by thin onion slices sautéed in butter until translucent. Serves about 6.

Medallions of Venison

This should be the second dish you make from a fresh-killed deer. (The first should be **Linda's Deer Liver***, page 82.) This recipe can be scaled up until you run out of backstrap.*

Cut six 1-inch-thick medallions from the center section of the left backstrap. Salt and pepper to taste. Put about a cup of flour in a plastic bag and add the venison. Shake bag to coat medallions with flour. Remove from bag.

Melt some bacon or deer fat, about 3 tablespoons more or less, in your skillet. (You can substitute canola oil, but you'll sacrifice flavor.) Place medallions in skillet, well separated, over medium high heat. Let cook without moving until blood shows through flour on top of medallion.

Flip over and cook for slightly less time on the other side. The secret here is to *not overcook*, or the medallions will be tough. Remove, place on hot serving platter to rest.

Now into the skillet toss a couple of handfuls of thin sliced onions and sauté until translucent. Remove onions from skillet, place over medallions. Into the skillet pour 1 cup semisweet red wine—Marsala works well here. Turn heat up and reduce wine by one-quarter to one-half, scraping with spatula to deglaze the pan.

Remove from heat, whisk in 2 tablespoons butter, and pour over the onions and medallions. Serve immediately on warm plates. Serves 2.

Lamb and Bamb with Port Wine Sauce

This is a dinner party signature dish that has never ceased to amaze and delight our guests.

1 leg of lamb, shank end removed
1 6- to 8-inch section backstrap of venison (about a
    pound or so)
2 sprigs each fresh rosemary, thyme, and sage
1 dozen juniper berries (optional)
6 cloves garlic, peeled and sliced lengthwise
olive oil
2 cups good quality port wine
3–4 beef bullets (page 68)
2 tablespoons unsalted butter

Bone, or have your butcher bone the leg of lamb. Save the bone for **Scotch Broth**. Place backstrap inside the boned leg of lamb. Surround backstrap with rosemary, thyme, sage, and, if you can find them, juniper berries. Close up roast and bind with cotton string.

Using a small pointed knife, make shallow slits in the surface of the lamb. Insert garlic slices into slits. Place lamb on baking rack in a large cast iron skillet. Drizzle a teaspoon or so of olive oil over the roast. Insert probe of meat thermometer into thickest part of roast. Be sure probe also penetrates the backstrap.

Place cast iron skillet containing racked roast in preheated 350-degree oven. Roast until internal temperature reaches 140 degrees for medium rare (recommended). Remove from oven. Let rest for 20 minutes, covered with a tent of foil.

Pour off excess fat from skillet. Deglaze the skillet with your best port wine—not the cheap cooking stuff you have on your *mise en place*. Reduce by about one-quarter. Add beef bullets. Stir them in over low heat.

Off heat, whisk in butter. Pour into heated sauce tureen or gravy tureen and keep warm.

Slice the now-rested roast, making sure each slice contains both lamb and venison. Arrange on warm serving platter. Pour some of the sauce over. Serve immediately with the sauce on the side. Use warm plates. Serves 6 to 8, depending on size of joint of lamb.

Accompaniments:

This dish goes especially well with **Oven Roasted Vegetables**, which can be done while the lamb roast is resting. Also serve **Wild Rice Casserole**, which can be made the day before and reheated. Consider one of the palate-cleansing salads (**Asian Pear with Fig** would be good here).

After everyone has repaired to the living room, serve a thin slice of chilled **Stanford Cheesecake** accompanied by your finest port or a snifter of your good brandy, and pass your humidor of fine cigars.

Wine Recommendation:

A high-quality California pinot or Cabernet goes well. We have an excellent local vintner, Robert Goodman. www.robertgoodmanwines.com

Venison or Any Other Red Meat Stew

This is a dish that I like to set on the wood stove and let simmer all day.

3 to 4 pounds of venison (or any other red meat— goat is especially good), cut into 1" chunks.
salt and pepper to taste
flour to dredge
3–4 tablespoons fat—beef, venison, or chicken—or you can use canola oil
dry red wine
stock

Salt and pepper meat chunks on all sides, then dredge with flour. You can do this in a bag, if you like. In a large cast iron skillet heat 3 to 4 tablespoons beef fat, venison fat, or chicken fat. If you don't have any of these, use canola oil, which works just as well and cuts some calories—and also some taste.

Brown meat on all sides. This will take 2 or 3 batches because you do *not* want to crowd the meat in the skillet.

As you remove the meat, drain it on paper towels, then place it in your cast iron Dutch oven. After the last batch of meat has left the skillet, deglaze the pan with a dry red wine. Pour the deglazing liquid into the Dutch oven. Add enough of the good stock you've made (see page 64) to bring the liquid level up to halfway on the meat. Bring to boil, cover, cut back to low simmer and leave on a back burner on your range or set it on your wood stove. Or you can put it in the oven at 325 degrees for 4 to 5 hours. Or you can use a slow cooker on top of the counter.

Check occasionally, adding stock or water to bring the liquid level to approximately half the height of the meat. Stir when you do this.

When the meat is fork-tender it is done. Remove meat, set aside, put the Dutch oven on the stove. Reduce liquid by one-quarter. Either skim residual fat off the surface or pour liquid into a gravy grease separator. Put meat back into Dutch oven. Pour degreased liquid over it. You are now in a holding pattern and can serve any time within the next hour

or so, or keep it warm in the oven. Serves 6 or more.
Leftovers are very good and keep very well when
vacuum sealed and frozen.

Accompaniments:

Serve with **Oven-Roasted Vegetables**, page 56.
Parsnip Mashed Potatoes, page 54.
Or polenta.

Variations:

Do this a day ahead of when you want to serve it. Put
it in the refrigerator. This will make it easy to pick
off the fat. It will also meld and increase the flavors.
About an hour or so before you're ready to serve,
reheat.

For as long as I've been hunting I've heard the
dispute as to whether it is better to age (hang)
venison and other red game meat, or to cut and
wrap it as it falls. After talking with many who
should know—the oldtime guides, the butchers
who work in game-producing communities, and
even a professionally trained chef—I've learned
that it does no good and may even harm the
flavor to hang game meat.

The professional chef went into a great deal of
scientific reasoning before finally expressing it
this basic way: Game meat, unlike beef and other
domestic meats, has very little fat. Consequently,
ageing does nothing to improve and may indeed
detract from its flavor and tenderness.

It seems to me that if you're a hunter, the
best way to secure tasty game meat for your
table is to bag—quickly—a younger animal
rather than going for the biggest rack. The
trophies may look good on your wall, but they
won't eat very well.

Savory Tender Goat, Venison, or Any Other Tough Meat

This recipe can also be made in a slow cooker on your kitchen counter. It produces a savory, tender concoction, especially when made with goat or mutton.

2 pounds goat, mutton, venison,
  or any other tough meat
salt and pepper to taste
2 tablespoons canola oil
12 garlic cloves, mashed
1 medium onion, chopped
1 green pepper, chopped
¼ cup sundried tomatoes
12 peppercorns
1 bay leaf
mayacoba beans (optional, see page 89)
bean water (optional)

Cut meat into slices, cubes, or steaks 1" thick. Sprinkle with salt and pepper; dry completely on paper towels.

In a cast iron Dutch oven, brown the meat, in small batches, in canola oil, setting aside pieces as they brown.

After all the meat has been browned and set aside, throw into the Dutch oven 12 or so garlic cloves that have been mashed; one medium onion, chopped; and one green pepper, chopped. Brown, adding more canola oil if necessary.

Remove vegetables from Dutch oven. Deglaze the Dutch oven with water or wine, any kind. Put everything back in Dutch oven, then throw in sundried tomatoes, peppercorns, and bay leaf. Add water or wine to cover halfway, put the lid on, bring to boil, then take heat back down to a very low simmer. Simmer slowly on stove or in the oven until meat is tender, 2 to 4 hours, checking meat occasionally with a fork.

Remove from oven; pull the meat out with pluckers and set aside. Strain the stock (throw away the vegetables or feed 'em to the chickens; they've done their job) and skim off excess fat or pour stock into a gravy grease separator. Pour degreased stock back into the Dutch oven, add 2 cups or so of the water that the beans have cooked in (see recipe below), and cook on top of stove until volume has been reduced by one-half.

Put cooked beans in serving dish (see recipe below), arrange the meat on top, and pour the reduced stock over. Serves 4.

Savory Mayacoba Beans

2 cups dried Mayacoba beans or baby limas
2 quarts warm water
1 teaspoon salt

Soak beans in warm water for 2 hours. Add salt, bring to rapid boil, reduce to a slow simmer with lid on. Cook to taste. Strain the beans. Pour 2 cups bean juice into Dutch oven with stock from meat. Reduce by half.

Very nice with cubed, steamed, salted and peppered **Chayote Squash and Fennel** (page 62).

Serve with **Whole Wheat Mountain Bread** (page 130).

Banana Kiwi Salad makes a nice accompaniment (page 114).

This makes a lovely dinner. Each of the dishes plays nicely against the others.

If you like the flavor of goat cheese, chances are you'll like goat meat. Elderly lamb (mutton to the Brits) is a passable substitute, but we feel that "the real thing" is best. Try a Mexican market and ask for chivo (**chee**-vo). They'll wonder how you found out.

Nothin' Fancy One-Skillet Dinner

This is a good dish to let simmer on the wood stove all afternoon.

2 pounds of a tough slab of meat: venison, goat,
   mutton, or beef bottom round
salt and pepper
sprinkle of flour
sprinkle of paprika
2 to 3 tablespoons of meat fat OR canola oil
½ cup water or any kind of wine you have handy

mirepoix:
1 medium onion, chopped
6 cloves of garlic, crushed
4 or 5 celery stalks, cut into pieces
any other vegetables that come to hand

dinner vegetables:
4 medium-sized potatoes, cut in chunks
2 medium-sized carrots, sliced diagonally

Salt and pepper the cut of meat. Dust with flour and paprika (optional). Get out your Grizzy #8, throw in 2 to 3 tablespoons of the fat that you've saved from other recipes. Heat until almost smoking, then throw in the chunk of seasoned meat and brown on all sides.

Pull meat out; set aside. Pour off excess fat. With skillet still on the fire, toss in the mirepoix: 1 medium onion, chopped; 6 cloves of garlic, crushed (these are essential); 4 or 5 celery stalks, cut into pieces; and any other vegetables you have in the refrigerator that you want to get rid of. Throw in ½ cup of water or any kind of wine you have handy and bring to steaming boil.

After the mirepoix vegetables have come to a steaming boil, put the meat back in on top of the veggies. Put on the lid, turn the heat to a very low simmer, or, at this point, set skillet on the wood stove. Let simmer 3 to 4 hours, replenishing liquid as necessary (don't let this go dry). This meat will never be fork-tender.

About three-quarters of an hour before you're ready to serve, add chunks of potatoes and carrots (the keepables) to the skillet and continue to simmer, covered. When potatoes and carrots are fork-tender, this dish is done.

Remove skillet from heat. With pluckers, remove meat, potatoes, and carrots; set aside. Strain what remains in the skillet. Throw away the now-spent vegetables—they've done their job. Return the strained sauce to the Grizzy. Return the potatoes and carrots (the keepables), and leave skillet off heat, covered.

After the meat has rested on a carving board for 10 minutes or so, slice it as thin as you can across the grain. Return sliced meat to skillet. Crank the heat up to a boil, then turn off heat, bring the skillet right to the table, set on a trivet, and serve.

This recipe will produce more than enough meat for 2 people, leaving a fine sufficiency for hash or **Creekside** (page 12) in the morning, or sandwiches for lunch.

Horseradish goes well with this. So does **Mountain Bread** (page 130), to slop up the juices.

Variations:

#1: Before serving, garnish with any type of cheese, Italian seasoning, garlic, parsley—anything that comes to hand.

#2: To save time and effort, you can serve this dish without removing the depleted vegetables. It will taste exactly the same but won't look as pretty.

Braised Goat (or Lamb) Shoulder Steaks

Savory and just slightly sweet, this dish is finger-lickin' good.

3 pounds goat shoulder (can use lamb in a pinch)
salt, pepper, and paprika to taste
2 tablespoons canola oil
½ cup sundried tomatoes, chopped
½ cup dried wild mushrooms (chanterelles if you can find them)

Cut the meat in ¾" slices. Bring meat to room temperature; sprinkle with salt, pepper, and paprika. Heat a cast-iron skillet with canola oil to just barely smoking. Throw the meat in, spacing widely. Brown deeply (about 5 minutes). Flip over, brown other side another 5 minutes or so. Remove and reserve. Put in the rest of the meat and do the same. Altogether, this will take about 20 minutes.

Deglaze the skillet with water. Put the meat back in, making sure the liquid is about half as high as the meat. Throw in the chopped sundried tomatoes and the dried mushrooms (chanterelles if you have them). Cover and cook on a low simmer for at least an hour.

Remove the lid, boil the liquid down (with meat still in) to a little less than a half. Remove the meat and set aside on your heated serving dish. Now kick the heat up and reduce the sauce to a fair consistency, whatever you like. Now it's your choice to either pour the sauce with the mushrooms over the meat or to strain it and then pour over the meat; either way it'll taste about the same.

Baby fresh sweet peppers (yellow, orange, and red) go well with this dish. Slice crosswise into ½" rounds, sauté in hot canola oil, tossing frequently. At the last minute toss in a little white vinegar to get a flambé. Serve with the goat.

Accompany with shell pasta, orzo, or polenta.

Ground Goat (or Lamb) Ragout

Monday night football provides my chance to fix dinner, the kind that can sit on the stove and be dipped into at half-time, catch as catch can. Here is one such dish that met with male approval at our house.

2 cups white beans
6 cups water
2 bay leaves
1 sprig fresh thyme
3 teaspoons Marigold bouillon powder
2 squirts Bragg's liquid amino seasoning
2 pieces kombu
1 tablespoon canola oil
1 large clove garlic, minced
1 pound ground goat (can use lamb if no goat available)
2 stalks celery, cut fine
3 carrots, cut fine
1 parsnip, cut fine
1 large pod guajillo chile

In medium saucepan, soak beans for 3 hours in 6 cups water. Add Marigold powder, bay leaves, thyme, kombu, and Bragg's and turn on the heat under saucepan till just short of a boil, then put it on low simmer for 1 hour. Add more water as necessary to keep beans covered.

In an 8" cast iron skillet, heat oil. Add garlic and stir until browned. Remove garlic and add to pan containing the beans. Brown the ground goat a little at a time, removing browned meat to saucepan. Pour fat off skillet, ladle a little of the bean water into skillet to deglaze, then pour the result back into the saucepan.

In a separate saucepan put the celery, carrots, and parsnip to boil in water sufficient to cover. When the carrots are tender, add vegetables to beans and meat mixture. Add guajillo chile, whole.

Simmer the whole savory mess until the beans are tender. Serves 4 to 6.

(Optional idea: add cauliflower florets during the last 10 minutes of cooking.)

Goat (or Lamb) Loaf

6 strips bacon
2 pounds ground goat or lamb
2 eggs
¾ cup old-fashioned oats
½ medium onion, minced
salt and pepper

Try out bacon in a #8 skillet. In a large bowl or a mixer, blend meat, eggs, oats, and onion, adding salt and pepper to taste. Line bottom of loaf pan with half of the bacon. Fill loaf pan with meat mixture, then add remaining strips of bacon on top. Bake 1 hour at 375 degrees. Remove from oven, let sit 10 minutes for flavor to absorb. Pour off excess fat. Slice and serve.

   Makes 6 generous servings

Bird(s) in Iron

Two words describe this recipe: low and slow.

1 medium chicken OR 1 large grouse
   OR 3 to 4 large quail
salt and pepper
2 tablespoons olive oil or canola oil
1 medium onion, chopped
6 cloves garlic, crushed
¾ cup chopped celery
1 bay leaf
sprig of fresh rosemary (optional)
½ cup dry white wine OR vermouth (optional)
1½ teaspoons lemon juice (juice of 1 fresh lemon)

Pat birds dry with a paper towel. Salt and pepper birds all over. In your large Dutch oven throw in olive oil. Heat to almost smoking, lay bird(s) in, breast side down, and brown on medium heat for approximately 5 minutes. Throw in onion, garlic, celery, bay leaf, and rosemary (optional).

After bird(s) have been browned breast-side, turn over, breast side up, and continue browning vegetables and back(s) of bird(s) over medium-high heat another 6 to 8 minutes. Pour in dry white wine or vermouth (optional).

Cover tightly. (If your lid does not fit really tightly, use aluminum foil to seal. This is important.) Put into preheated 250-degree oven.

After 1 hour, check temperature of bird(s) with instant-read thermometer. Thickest part of breast should read 160. Smaller bird(s) will probably be done around now; larger bird(s) may have to go back in for another 30 or 40 minutes. At that point when the birds are done, if you want crispier skin, remove the lid and place under broiler for about 3 to 5 minutes. Keep a close eye out because they can burn easily.

When bird(s) are done, remove from oven and let rest (covered with a tent of foil) on cooling rack over carving board. You will now have in the Dutch oven about 1 cup of very flavorful stock. Into a gravy grease separator, strain stock through a medium strainer, mashing the vegetables to get maximum through-put. Discard the vegetables.

Let stock sit in the gravy grease separator to give fat an opportunity to rise to the top. Pour defatted stock into a small saucepan, set over low heat, and add the juice of one lemon (1½ teaspoons lemon juice).

After the bird(s) have rested at least 20 minutes, carve, set on rimmed serving platter, and pour degreased stock over. If dinner isn't quite ready, this will hold in the oven a while. Serves 4.

Accompaniments:

baked yams (the *jus* goes especially well over yams)
baked potatoes
Parsnip Mashed Potatoes (page 54)
baked squash

Quick and Easy Chicken Over Shells

1½ pound boned skinless chicken breast
1 pound large shell pasta
salt to taste
2 tablespoons canola oil
½ cup Parmesan or other hard cheese, shredded
1 cup sweet baby peppers
1 cup stock (chicken or beef)
Italian seasoning to taste (optional)

Cook pasta according to package directions. *Al dente* is usually 9 minutes boiling time.

While pasta is cooking, cube chicken breast. Dry on paper towel. Heat canola oil in #8 cast iron skillet until just barely smoking. Throw in chicken cubes. Saute on high heat 1 minute. Turn heat down, pour in 1 cup stock, cover, let simmer for 4 minutes. Remove everything to another container. Turn heat up to high on the #8. Add 1 tablespoon of canola oil, throw in sweet baby peppers and sauté briefly.

About this time the pasta should be ready. Drain and place in serving dish. Pour in chicken and sauce and throw the peppers over it. Sprinkle with Parmesan and a little Italian seasoning if you want.

Serve with Parmesan cheese and a good bread on the side. A nice Chianti or Merlot goes well with this; keep it economical—no need for expensive here. Serves 4.

Chicken Thighs a la Marsala (and Vermouth)

6 skin-on chicken thighs
salt and pepper to taste
1 small onion, sliced fine
1 clove garlic, minced
¼ cup sundried tomatoes
½ cup dried wild mushrooms
½ cup Marsala wine
¼ cup dry vermouth

Soak tomatoes and dried wild mushrooms in hot water to cover. Dry chicken thighs on paper towel. Salt and pepper to taste. Heat the Grizzy #8, throw in thighs, skin-side down. Crank up the heat and brown thighs on all sides until your wife yells at you that they're smoking. Pull out thighs with a plucker, set 'em on the dish you're gonna be eatin off of, pour the grease off the skillet and set it back on the fire (the skillet, not the grease). Put the chicken joints back in, with the undersides next to the skillet. Maybe 5 to 8 minutes. Pull 'em off again.

Leave whatever grease there is in the skillet—there won't be much—throw in some chopped onions and chopped garlic, turn the fire up, sauté for 2 or 3 minutes, until onions and garlic release their juices.

Throw onions and garlic on top of the chicken that is out of the pot. Put skillet back on stove, turn heat off.

Deglaze the skillet with ½ cup of Marsala wine. Throw everything back into the skillet, bring to a boil. Cut heat back to low, put a lid on it. Whenever you feel like it, throw in sundried tomatoes and dried mushrooms that have been soaking in Marsala wine. Put the lid on again, let it simmer for 20 minutes or so, throw in the vermouth. Pull off the lid, crank the heat up a little and let the sauce reduce: this gets flavor into it. Turn the heat off and let it sit.

Serve over linguine or fettuchine *al dente*. Serves 2 or 3.

Chicken Breast Over Fettuccine

This chicken cooks very fast. Don't overdo it or you'll dry it out.

½ breast skinless, boneless chicken cut into 1"
   chunks
1–2 tablespoons canola oil
¼ cup vermouth or dry white wine
¼ pound fettuccine cooked according to package
   directions (also see Pasta Pointers,
   page 95)
1–2 tablespoons olive oil (enough to coat the pasta)
¼ cup Parmesan or Romano cheese
   or 2 tablespoons grated Sap Sago cheese
salt and pepper to taste

Dry the chicken with paper towels. Heat oil until almost smoking. Quickly sauté dry chicken chunks in the oil, no more than a minute or so. Turn heat to low. Pour off excess fat. Return pan to stove.

Add vermouth or white wine and stir briefly. Cover and let simmer for 5 minutes.

Turn heat off. Let rest, covered, another few minutes.
Pour everything over cooked fettuccine. Add olive
oil, cheese, and salt and pepper to taste. Toss to mix.
Serve on warm plates. Serves 2. Can be scaled up for
more diners.

Pasta Pointers

1 pound dry pasta
5 quarts cold water
2 teaspoons salt (to prevent pasta from sticking)

Add salt to water. Bring to a rapid boil. Add
pasta, stirring with a long wooden spoon.

When everything comes back to a rapid boil, start
the timing according to package directions. This
is where your kitchen timer comes in very handy;
you don't want to overcook or undercook pasta. I
usually shoot for the *al dente* time on the package.

Stir the pasta continually for the allotted time:
this is important to prevent sticking. Adjust
the heat to keep the pot at a rapid boil without
boiling over.

When the timer rings, strain the pasta, saving
the water for use in making bread, stock, or soup.
Do not rinse pasta. Immediately throw drained
pasta into a heated ceramic serving bowl. Toss
with olive oil to coat. Your pasta is now ready
to serve or go on to the next step in any of the
recipes.

Always serve pasta on warm dishes.

Chicken Cacciatore

I have also done this with rabbit, squirrel, and coon. Maybe that's why they call it "Hunter's Style." Though I've never done it, I imagine turkey would work in this dish, as well. The baby sweet peppers are a worthy addition, for they lend color and flavor to the dish. This dish is very accommodating of your personal cooking whims; don't be afraid to experiment.

dark meat of one large chicken
3 tablespoons canola oil
1 medium onion, peeled and chopped medium dice
8 cloves garlic, peeled, crushed, and chopped
    medium dice
4–5 baby sweet peppers, chopped medium dice
    (optional)
½ cup Marsala wine
1 (15-ounce) can Italian-style pear tomatoes
½ pound fresh mushrooms
OR 4–6 ounces dried wild mushrooms, reconstituted
¼ cup sun-dried tomatoes, chopped large dice
¼ teaspoon allspice

Disjoint the dark chicken meat. Remove excess fat and excess skin. Be sure to leave a fair amount of skin, for it contributes flavor.

In a #8 cast-iron skillet for which you have a lid, bring 2 tablespoons of the oil almost to smoking. Brown the chicken parts on all sides. This may take more than one pass through the skillet, since you don't want to crowd the pieces when browning.

Remove chicken from skillet to serving dish, pour off excess fat from skillet, throw in the onions and garlic, and sauté until the onions are translucent. If you're using the optional peppers, add them at this point.

Remove vegetables from skillet; put them over the chicken in the serving dish. Deglaze the skillet with a few tablespoons of Marsala. Return everything to skillet.

Add drained canned tomatoes. (If you can't find the Italian style, just use regular and add about 2 tablespoons Italian seasoning.)

If you are using reconstituted dried mushrooms, throw them in now. (If you're using fresh mushrooms, they go in later.) Add sun-dried tomatoes.

Now crank up the heat and reduce the liquids to about halfway up the chicken. Turn heat to a low simmer and cover skillet. Cook until chicken is tender but not falling off the bone. Depending on the size and toughness of the bird, this could be anywhere from 30 to 45 minutes. After 30 minutes, check with fork.

Before serving, add chopped fresh mushrooms if you're using them. Cook a few minutes longer.

Off heat, stir to mix ingredients. Sprinkle with allspice. Serve, or cover and hold. Serves 4.

Accompaniments:
any kind of pasta (see page 99)
polenta
Parsnip Mashed Potatoes (page 54)
Parsley Potatoes (page 53)
Quick and Easy Garlic Bread (page 133)

What's that old canard? "It tastes just like chicken."

"Well," one might ask, "What does chicken taste like?"

To that I would reply, with some authority, that chicken tastes like . . . rattlesnake.

Some years ago when I lived on the Whistlespit, we had an overabundance of rattlers.

Bulldozer Betty was down tending the garden she used to sharecrop. She yelled, "Matt, Matt, bring your gun, there's a big rattler down here!"

I grabbed the pistol I kept in the outdoor kitchen—loaded with #6 shot—and ran down and dispatched the beast.

It was over five feet long.

Rattlesnake is an excellent white meat. Use it in any recipe that calls for chicken breast.

Adzuki Beans, Sausage, and Polenta

For this dish, make your usual amount of polenta in your usual manner. After you have spread it over the mixture in the loaf pan, you should have plenty left over for polenta hash or grits. This is not at all a fancy dinner, but it is hearty, satisfying, and different enough to be intriguing

1 cup adzuki beans (or any other small red beans)
2 quarts cold water
2 tablespoons canola oil
1 large Italian sausage, about ¼ pound
¼ cup Marsala wine
2 tablespoons sun-dried tomatoes, chopped fine
polenta enough to cover cast-iron bread loaf pan
2 tablespoons Gorgonzola or other stinky cheese

Throw adzuki beans into water. Bring to boil; simmer until just barely *al dente*, 30 minutes to an hour or so, depending on age and composition of beans. Drain, reserving bean stock. This is very flavorful stock, which you will probably want to add to your other concoctions.

While the beans are simmering, in a cast iron skillet heat canola oil to almost smoking. Brown the whole Italian sausage. Deglaze the pan with Marsala. Remove sausage from skillet, slice diagonally, and set aside.

Pour beans into a cast iron loaf pan. (If you don't have a cast iron loaf pan, you can use any other loaf pan.) Lay sausage slices on top of beans. Pour deglazed liquid over all. Sprinkle chopped sun-dried tomatoes over. Pour polenta over to fill pan. Place in preheated 325-degree oven for about 1 hour. Remove from oven. Set on cooling rack for half an hour so juices can resorb.

Directly before serving, sprinkle Gorgonzola and ½ tablespoon chopped dried tomatoes over the top. Put under broiler for maybe 5 minutes or so. Keep a close eye so it doesn't scorch.

Serve on warm plates. Serves 2 with leftovers. You can double this if you have 2 loaf pans.

Variation: Kick up the interest by substituting hot Italian sausage and adding a few guajillo chiles. Serve with Tabasco.

Sausage and Clams over Pasta

When the boys were but pups, some days we would come home cold, wet, and hungry from a day of sailing or hunting or fishing. The boys would complain that they were hungry. I would throw a pot on the stove and proceed to cook this dish. To this day, as men now in their forties, they ask for it.

It can be made equally as well with frozen sausages. Just toss frozen sausages in the boiling water, and when they thaw sufficiently, pull them out of their plastic wrappers and toss them back into the boiling water and let them parboil that way.

The shells are best, for they make tidy little boats that hold the sauce and the clams quite congenially. No other form of pasta performs this task quite as well.

1 pound large shells pasta
1½ pound raw Italian sausages, mild or hot
2 (6½ ounce) cans chopped clams
½ cup extra dry vermouth
1 tablespoon canola oil
sprinkling of dried parsley or Italian seasoning
shredded Parmesan to taste

Set your pot to boiling and cook the shells per package directions (usually 12 minutes).

While pasta is cooking, place your raw sausages in a #8 skillet and add ¼ inch of water. Over medium heat, sauté your sausages for about 10 minutes, turning occasionally.

About now, your pasta should be done. Drain pasta and put in serving dish.

Remove parboiled sausages from skillet and set aside. Dump clams and clam juice into skillet. A miniscule amount of water will remain from parboiling the sausages. Add ½ cup extra dry vermouth. Crank heat up to high and bring to boil, stirring, for less than a minute. Pour over pasta.

Slice blanched sausages diagonally. Throw the sausage slices in the skillet and brown the sausages in a little canola oil. Place browned sausage slices over the pasta and clams. Garnish with a sprinkling of parsley or Italian seasoning, for color.

Sprinkle with Parmesan or Sap Sago. Serves 4.

Skillet Poached Salmon or Steelhead

This produces fish the way it would be served in a fine restaurant: pink on the inside, but warm and flaking easily to a fork. If you like your fish well-done, go find another cookbook.

2 medium carrots, sliced diagonally
6 stalks celery, cut to 6" lengths
1 medium onion, sliced
2 cups dry white wine
1 pound salmon or steelhead filets or steaks
sprinkling of lemon pepper seasoning
sprinkling dried or fresh dill

Place onions, carrots, and celery in cast iron skillet. Pour in wine. Bring to boil. Reduce by one-quarter.

Lay filets or steaks of fish on top of mirepoix. Sprinkle lemon pepper over. Cover; cook on medium low heat for 5 minutes. (This assumes that no part of the fish is more than 1" thick. If it is thicker or less thick, adjust cooking time.)

Remove fish from skillet and place on warm serving dish. Increase heat under skillet to a boil; reduce stock just a little. Pour stock through strainer over fish. Sprinkle dill weed and lemon pepper over. Serve immediately to warm plates. Serves 2.

Accompaniments:

Serve over brown basmati rice surrounded by fresh steamed asparagus spears or broccolini.

Steelhead and Black-Eyed Peas

This sounds complicated but is really quite simple. The black-eyed peas are a surprisingly adroit companion for the steelhead, echoing its silky succulence. This will work for steelhead or salmon or any red-meat fish you bring home, but the dish is at its best with steelhead, whose delicacy it sets off nicely.

1 cup dried black-eyed peas
water to double the volume of peas
¼ cup salt pork
1 tablespoon olive oil
5 or 6 sweet baby peppers, chopped
1 pound steelhead (or salmon) filets
1 tablespoon olive oil
dash lemon pepper
2 tablespoons dry white wine or vermouth

First prepare the peas:

In a small saucepan, bring peas to boil in water, then turn down to simmer.

In a small cast iron skillet (#5), parboil about ¼ cup salt pork, changing water twice. Add drained, parboiled salt pork to simmering peas. In same small skillet, sauté chopped baby peppers in olive oil. Add to peas, which are still simmering. When peas are tender (half an hour to 45 minutes), drain, reserving liquid. Put peas in a warm dish and hold in a warm oven. Slightly reduce juice from peas in the small saucepan the peas cooked in. Set on back burner and keep warm.

Now prepare the steelhead:

Pour olive oil into cast iron skillet (a #10 or a #8 for which you have a lid) and heat skillet over medium flame. Add fish to skillet, skin side down. Sprinkle a little lemon pepper on the fish. Cover and let steam for two minutes. Use a timer. Add wine or vermouth. Stir and cover. Turn heat down and let cook another two minutes. Remove fish to warm platter.

Pour reduced pea juices over the steelhead. Serve on warm platter to warm dishes. Serves 2.

Accompaniments:

A few stalks of lightly steamed asparagus or broccolini would be good with this.

Prawns and Scallops over Orzetto

Quick and delicious. Don't be misled by the simplicity of this recipe. Its results are superb.

1 cup orzetto
4 cups boiling water
1 teaspoon salt
½ pound large prawns
4 jumbo scallops
1 cup white wine (primo grigio, chardonnay, etc.) or vermouth
½ large head garlic, peeled, pressed, and chopped
1 tablespoons butter
1 tablespoon olive oil

Into 4 cups boiling water put one cup orzetto and salt. Bring back to boil, cook uncovered for 8 minutes, stirring frequently. Strain orzetto, reserving stock for whatever machinations you may later have in mind.

Peel the prawns. Throw shells into sauté pan (you can use a Grizzy #8 or whatever) along with garlic and white wine. Cover and simmer over low heat for 10 minutes or so. Add peeled prawns and scallops, cook

for another 3 minutes. With a plucker, remove the prawns and scallops and set over the previously cooked orzetto.

Lower the heat a bit; throw in butter, a little olive oil, and sauté over low heat until butter melts—you don't want to burn the butter. Put orzetto into a warm casserole and place prawns and scallops on top. Strain pan juices and pour over. Toss and serve to warm plates.

Serves 2 generously. Easily doubled or tripled.

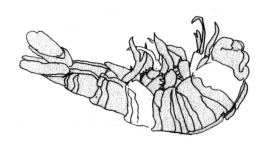

Poached Scallops

You can also make this using prawns or oysters in addition to the scallops. If you don't have white wine or dry vermouth, you can substitute clam broth. A low-sodium chicken broth would work. If you don't have any of these, water will work, though you'll lose some flavor.

1 pound large sea scallops
3 stalks celery, sliced lengthwise
1 medium carrot, sliced lengthwise
1 small onion, sliced
1 bay leaf
1 cup dry white wine or dry vermouth

Place all ingredients except scallops in a skillet. Bring liquid to a boil. Cover and simmer for 5 minutes. Remove lid, set the scallops on top of the vegetables, bring back to simmer. Cover and simmer for 5 minutes. Uncover. Using a sharp knife, cut into one of the scallops to see if it's done to your taste. For best flavor, scallops should still be translucent on the inside. Simmer longer if necessary.

Remove scallops with a plucker, place on warm plate. Strain liquid, pour it over the scallops, and throw away the vegetables, which have done their job. If you like the flavor, season with lemon pepper. Serves 2.

This goes well over a bed of brown basmati rice. Also good with pasta.

Calamari Steaks

This is a good substitute for abalone, which can be very difficult to come by. As with abalone, the secret is to not overcook the calamari. If you do overcook and your steaks toughen up, the fall-back position is to pour off any oil, put steaks back in the pan, put in a cup of white wine or vermouth, cover and let simmer for 20 minutes. This also makes an excellent dish.

2 eggs, beaten
1 tablespoon cold water
sprinkling of flour
1 pound calamari steaks
1 cup panko bread crumbs
2 tablespoons canola oil

Beat eggs and water together. Sprinkle flour on both sides of steaks. Dip floured steaks in egg mixture. Dredge in panko crumbs.

Heat oil in cast iron skillet until almost smoking. Place breaded steaks in skillet. Adjust heat so oil is not smoking.

Cook *no more than two minutes* on one side. Use your timer. Turn over and cook one minute on the other side. Serve immediately on warm plates.

Depending on the size of your skillet, you may have to run two or three batches. Don't crowd them. Serves 2.

Panko Pancakes

If you have beaten eggs and panko crumbs left over, add a little milk and then refrigerate the mixture overnight. Next morning the crumbs will have absorbed the wet ingredients and will have puffed up considerably. Now heat some olive oil or a little butter in a cast iron skillet and drop this mixture into it about a quarter-cup at a time. Makes the nicest little pancakes you ever ate.

Abalone Steaks

It has oft been said—and having brought home a few myself, I truly believe it to be so—that the calories expended in the getting of the abalone will never be replenished by the eating thereof. I will not bore you with the steps that were necessary to set the popped, gutted, and trimmed mollusk before you. Let us simply proceed from that point. First off, this is a meal that the cook does not even put in the pan until everyone is seated. He serves each diner as each abalone steak comes out of the pan. The cook does not sit down and eat his own portion until the last diner has been satisfied.

(If you are fortunate enough to have the trimmings from the abalone, reserve them: They make an excellent **Abalone Chowder**.*)*

1 7-inch abalone for each two diners
3 eggs
3 tablespoons water
dash of pepper
2 cups fine bread crumbs
2 tablespoons butter
lemon wedges

Using a very sharp slicing knife, cut the creature into ⅜-inch slices. Pound slices gently with an abalone pounder to about ¼ inch.

Beat eggs; and water and mix well. Coat abalone steaks in beaten egg mixture. Dredge in bread crumbs.

Over medium flame, heat 2 tablespoons butter in a large cast iron skillet. Now, here comes the critical point of abalone cooking: Cook coated abalone steaks in hot butter *no more than 30 seconds on one side*. Flip and cook another 30 seconds. Overcook it and it'll be as tough as your wetsuit.

As steaks come out of the skillet, serve immediately on warm plates. Serve with lemon wedges, tossed green salad, and a good store-bought sourdough bread.

Wine Recommendations:

A good California Chardonnay is perfect with this.

Chanterelle Prawns and Scallops

The key ingredient to the flavor of this dish is the chanterelles. Nothing else is quite the same. The chanterelles work very nicely with the prawns, and produce a delicately flavored sauce that the fettuccine absorbs to fine effect.

olive oil to coat fettuccine
¼ pound fettuccine, cooked *al dente* **according to package directions**
1 cup dried chanterelle mushrooms (see Resources)
1 cup very hot water
1 tablespoon olive oil
3 stalks celery, sliced lengthwise
1 medium onion, sliced
1 carrot, sliced lengthwise
1 cup dry white wine or dry vermouth
½ pound scallops
½ pound prawns, peeled (reserve shells)
¼ cup grated Parmesan

Cook fettuccine according to package directions. Cover cooked fettuccine with olive oil to coat. Set aside and keep warm.

Pour hot water over dried chanterelles; set aside. In a #10 skillet, heat olive oil. Throw in vegetables and wine, along with shells from prawns. Bring to boil. Reduce heat to simmer; cover and let simmer 10 minutes. To skillet add prawns and scallops. Bring back to boil; reduce to low simmer, cover, and cook 5 minutes.

Pluck out prawns and scallops. Set over fettuccine cooked *al dente* according to package directions.

Strain liquid into a small (2-quart) saucepan. Strain liquid from mushrooms into saucepan. Reduce by approximately one-quarter. Add mushrooms. Bring back to boil for a minute or so. Pour over prawns, scallops, and fettucinne.

Toss with grated Parmesan. Serve immediately on warm dishes. Serves 2.

Spicy Whiskey Stew

Good for any tough red meat, but goat is especially delicious if you can get it. Bear would also work. Use beef if that's all you've got. It'll still be tender and tasty (and spicy).

2 teaspoons salt
1 teaspoon black pepper
1 cup flour
¼ teaspoon cayenne pepper
1 tablespoon chili flakes and seeds
2 pounds tough red meat, cut into 1" chunk
½ cup canola oil
1 cup cheap whiskey
1 cup baby sweet peppers, sliced and diced

Place salt, pepper, flour, cayenne pepper, chili flakes and seeds in a plastic bag. Add portions of meat to bag, a few at a time, and shake to coat with flour/spice mixture, then remove meat pieces from bag and toss in a large sieve to remove excess flour. Return excess flour/spice siftings back to plastic bag. Repeat process, using only a few pieces of meat at a time.

In a large cast iron skillet, heat 2 tablespoons oil until nearly smoking, then brown chunks of meat on all sides in small batches, adding a little oil for each new batch. Do not crowd the meat or it will steam rather than brown. As meat is browned, remove it to a cast iron dutch oven.

When all the meat has been browned, deglaze the skillet with whiskey. Reduce by half, pour over meat in dutch oven, then add water up to about one-half the height of the meat.

Add sliced fresh peppers. Bring to boil on top of stove, then reduce to a low simmer. If you have a wood stove, cover and let it continue to cook at a very low simmer. Otherwise, cover and put it in a 325 degree oven for about 3 hours. Check after 1 hour, adding more liquid if necessary. Part of this liquid could be more whiskey, if you wish. Cook until meat is tender, which could take as long as 3 hours. Serves 4–6.

Serve with boiled potatoes and onions, or cooked dried mayacoba beans. Also, if you're serving any sissies, serve with yogurt or sour cream as a side dish, to cut the bite.

Thoughts on Chili

First let me state that I am not going to give you my recipe, which is locked in my safe, or any other recipe for chili. If I may be excused for a little bragging, the recipe locked in the safe took second place in a large Marin County chili cook-off (first place went to the legendary San Francisco Fire Department).

There are literally thousands—maybe millions—of ways to make chili. To me, the first basic of a good chili is very lean, tough meat. I have used venison, bear, coon, horse, and other things you probably don't want to know about. All have produced good chili.

In addition to the tough, stringy meat, you need tomatoes, tomato sauce, chili peppers, cayenne pepper, and masa harina.

I make my chili without beans. I make my chili hot. With the chili I like to serve beans, usually pintos or red beans, that have been seasoned to the mild side. That way, those eating your chili can combine the hot chili carne with the bland beans to satisfy their personal compression ratio.

Usually I also serve **Corn Bread** (page 132) and provide toppings of shredded sharp Cheddar cheese, chopped onions, and maybe some sour cream.

I told you I wasn't going to give you a recipe, but you've got enough ideas here to start from scratch and experiment, which is what chili-building is all about.

Good luck in your next chili cook-off.

A word about dinner salads, as we see them:

$\mathcal{H}$ere is your opportunity to balance the dusky, carnal flavors of Matt's meat dishes with a bright, sparkly palate-cleanser. In our opinion, these composed fresh-fruit salads need no dressings, for we consider them all the more appealing if you let the flavors of the fruits, nuts, and greens speak for themselves.

However, if a naked salad seems to you somehow unfinished, consider topping everything with a discreet drizzle of a low-fat fruit-flavored yogurt. Piña colada, lemon burst, or key lime pie are the flavors we favor. Or for an offbeat surprise, try dabs of peanut satay sauce, or **Honey Mustard Dressing.**

It's true that composing a dinner salad takes more work than assembling a compendium of greens and goodies in one large bowl. It's true that composed salads take up refrigerator space in multiples limited only by the number of your dinner guests. And it's true that separate, composed salads demand their own living room on your dinner table.

But consider them an opportunity to creatively complement the flavors of the meat entree. Look upon them as your artistic signature upon the dinner, as distinctive and colorful as the table you so carefully set. See them as a chance to add wit and whimsey to your meal.

You may not need a separate dessert; just save your salad for the end of the meal, in the Continental fashion, as we do.

"Oh, what a pretty salad!" your guests may exclaim. And they'll know it was made just for them.

Banana Kiwi Salad

This salad needs no dressing other than the coconut. Let the fruit flavors speak for themselves.

For 4 salads:

2 cups fresh baby spinach
2 bananas, sliced crosswise in thin slices
4 ripe kiwis, peeled and sliced
½ cup sweetened baker's coconut

Arrange ½ cup baby spinach on each salad plate. Distribute thin banana slices in a circle on each plate, leaving space in the center. Lay kiwi slices in a fan at the center of the circle. Sprinkle 2 tablespoons coconut over each.

Particularly good with the recipe for tough meat (**Savory Tender Goat, Venison, or Any Other Tough Meat,** page 88).

Fennel, Fig, and Fuji Salad

If you can't find dried Calimyrna figs, dried Mission figs will work. But if you can find **fresh** *figs of any type, oh frabjous day! This salad doesn't really need a dressing. Let the fruits carry the dish.*

For every 2 salads:

bed of fresh mixed herbs
1 Fuji apple, cored, sliced crosswise about ⅛" thick
4 dried Calimyrna figs, quartered lengthwise
4 very thin slices fresh fennel, cut from the bulb
2 tablespoons sliced almonds

On each salad plate, lay a bed of fresh mixed herbs. On top of the herbs, on each plate place 4 of the cored apple slices, overlapping slices slightly. In the cored-out center of each apple slice, put 2 pieces of the dried fig quarters.

Garnish each plate with 2 fennel slices, cut into slivers. Sprinkle 1 tablespoon sliced almonds over each salad.

Orange Avocado Pinwheel Salad

Quick, easy, colorful, and tasty, this is the composed salad I turn to most often.

For every 2 salads:

fresh mixed spring herbs
**1 large navel orange, peeled and separated into
   segments**
1 ripe avocado, peeled and sliced vertically
4 cubes candied ginger, cut fine
1 tablespoon slivered almonds (optional)

Strew each plate with a bed of mixed herbs.

On each plate lay half of the orange segments; shape them in a pinwheel fanning out from the center. (You'll usually have five for each plate.)

Cut the avocado into as many vertical slices as you have orange segments. Distribute in the spaces between the fanned-out orange segments so that orange alternates with avocado.

Scatter cut ginger over all. Top with slivered almonds if desired. Serves 2.

Orange Flower Salad

Sometimes you want to present a salad that not only tastes good, but also looks pretty. This one is colorful as well as delicious.

For 4 salads:

mixed baby spring greens
4 ripe navel oranges
¼ cup (or less) pine nuts
¼ cup dried cranberries or dried cherries
8–12 thin slices fresh fennel

Lay a thin bed of mixed baby greens on each salad plate. Now peel oranges and remove any membrane clinging to the outside. For each salad, start at the middle of one end of the peeled orange and carve a thin spiral as long as you can make before it breaks of its own weight. You should be able to get about three of these per orange.

Fold this spiral piece in on itself to resemble a flower. Drop about half a dozen pine nuts into the center of each flower. Arrange the fennel slices to resemble foliage surrounding the flowers. Decorate with dried cranberries or cherries where you deem appropriate to complete the picture. No dressing is needed; the fruits speak for themselves.

Makes 4 composed salads.

Variation:

Compose a bed of fresh herbs. Allowing one orange per plate, peel oranges and carefully separate slices so they fan out at the top but remain connected at the bottom. Place on bed of herbs, placing 20 or so dried cranberries in the center. Arrange very thin slices of fennel or jicama between the orange segments, radiating outwards toward the edge of the plate.

If the accompanying dishes have any spicy component, drizzle your choice of low-fat fruit-flavored yogurt discreetly around the orange "flower." The yogurt will help cut the "burn" of paprika, cayenne, or other spices in any accompanying dish, while the fruit flavor can complement the main dish ("lemon burst" or "orange crème" yogurt for fish, for example).

Grapes and Gorgonzola

Fussy but fun. Tastes good, too. Your kids will enjoy helping you compose these little "bunches of grapes."

leaf lettuce, red or green
red or green seedless grapes
chow mein noodles
crumbles of gorgonzola cheese

For each salad, lay on the plate one large leaf of lettuce. Use green lettuce for red grapes, red lettuce for green grapes.

Destem grapes and lay on lettuce leaf in a pattern resembling a bunch of grapes. Add chow mein noodles at strategic intervals to resemble grape twigs. Sprinkle gorgonzola crumbles sparingly over grapes.

Serves as many as you have materials, time, and patience for.

Tangy Vegetable Salad

This refreshing salad can substitute as your vegetable side dish.

1 small package frozen mixed vegetables
½ cup muffaletta
4 medium-sized slicing tomatoes
mixed spring greens
or
fresh arugula, if available

Place frozen mixed vegetables in a medium bowl. In the microwave, heat vegetables per package instructions (if in doubt, undercook). Cool. Chill in refrigerator 1 hour.

When ready to serve, toss with muffaletta. Cut each tomato into 8 wedges. Arrange on a bed of mixed spring greens (or arugula, if available). Spoon vegetable/muffaletta mix into the center of the tomato wedges.

Serves 4.

Tropical Fruit Salad

For each two salads, use the following:

spring mix salad greens
1 banana, sliced lengthwise
1 ripe mango, sliced
1 ripe avocado, sliced
2 tablespoons slivered almonds
1 tablespoon sweetened baker's coconut
2 cubes candied ginger, minced fine

On salad plates, create a thin bed of mixed greens. Slice banana in half lengthwise, then in half again crosswise. For each salad, place two of these slices on the bed of greens, arranging the bananas like opposing parentheses at the outer edges of the plate.

Between the banana strips, place slices of mango alternating with slices of avocado. In a small bowl put the almonds, coconut, and candied ginger; toss to mix. Distribute this topping over each salad.

Serves 2.

Crusty Tropical Salad

What, you've never seen a crust in a salad before?

6 graham crackers
½ cup macadamia nuts, chopped fine
½ cup baker's coconut
3-4 tablespoons butter
2 ripe mangoes, peeled and sliced
¼ cup ripe pineapple, sliced
mixed baby spring greens

First, make the crust. Put graham crackers in a small Zip-loc bag and smash, then roll them into fine crumbs with a rolling pin. To the bag add chopped nuts and coconut. Shake bag to mix well.

Melt butter in a small cast-iron skillet (a #5 is about right). Swirl to coat sides. Use a pastry brush to coat upper parts of the sides.

Pour contents of Zip-loc bag into skillet and stir with a fork until the mixture has taken up the melted butter evenly. With your fingers, shape buttered mixture into a pie crust in the skillet. Bake in preheated 425-degree oven for about 8 minutes. Watch it carefully; you want it to brown but not burn.

Remove from oven, set aside on rack until skillet is cool to the touch, then refrigerate for a couple of hours.

Meanwhile, cut sliced pineapple and mango slices into thin squares about ½ inch on all sides. Put fruit into a small ceramic bowl, stir to mix thoroughly, and refrigerate while the crust is chilling. This gives the flavors time to blend nicely.

When you're ready to serve, make a bed of greens on each salad plate. Remove skillet from refrigerator and carefully cut crust into 4 pieces. Run a knife around the sides of the skillet to free the crust. With a pie spatula, gently ease each piece of crust out of the skillet and onto the salad greens. Don't fret if it falls apart; don't worry if some of it crumbles: as long as some of it holds together to receive the fruit mix, Bob's your uncle.

Onto each "pie crust" spoon one-quarter of the chilled, mixed fruit. Sprinkle any loose crumbs over the fruit. Serves 4. Let your guests decide whether it's salad or dessert.

Bosc and Brie with Toasted Almonds

Like **Crusty Tropical Salad**, *this one can function as either salad or dessert. You'll want to save it for last, the way you might save fruit and cheese. If you're watching calories, choose the Neufachtel, but if flavor is your primary concern, indulge in the Brie. It's a perfect partner for the Bosc pear.*

For every 2 salads:

mixed baby spring greens or mixed herb salad greens
2 large leaves radicchio
1 Bosc pear
2 melon-ball scoops Brie cheese (can substitute Neufchatel)
¼ cup toasted almonds, chopped

On salad plates, make a thin bed of mixed baby greens, leaving the center only very thinly covered, if at all. Place on the center a large leaf of fresh radicchio (separate it from the head carefully, so it stays in one piece),

Slice the pear lengthwise. For each half, scoop out the core with a melon ball scoop. Nestle pear half in the radicchio. Slice the pear once more, lengthwise, to slightly separate the pieces.

Place scoops of Brie (or Neufchatel) cheese in the cavities of the pears. Sprinkle chopped toasted almonds over all.

Serves 2, but scales up easily in multiples of two.

Apple, Tangerine, and Banana with Peanut Satay Dabs

The peanut satay sauce makes this salad special. It provides a harmonizing, common flavor ground among the three fruits.

For every 2 salads:

bed of fresh spring mixed greens
2 Clementine tangerines
1 Gala apple (can use Fuji), unpeeled
2 small bananas
1 tablespoon peanut satay sauce

Around the outer rim of the salad plate, lay a wreath of spring greens. Set aside.

Peel tangerine and separate into segments. On your work area, distribute these segments in a circle, outer edges of the segments facing up. Leave a space about 3" in diameter in the middle of this circle of tangerine segments.

Now cut through the apple crosswise, slicing off a chunk as tall as the tangerine segments are long.

Quarter this chunk of apple, cutting away stem and any core portions. Count the tangerine segments; slice the apple chunk into as many pieces are there are tangerine segments. Intersperse apple slices between pieces of tangerine. Move fruit wreath onto salad plate.

Cut banana into fine crosswise slices. Lay a few banana slices in center of fruit wreath. Distribute remaining banana slices around perimeter of wreath.

Dab peanut satay sauce around fruit on wreath. Place a small dab in the center of each banana slice. For a more pleasing presentation, turn banana slices sauce-side down. The unexpected peanut taste will provide a pleasant surprise.

Asian Pear, Fig, and Bean Sprout Salad with Honey Mustard Dressing

This salad plays off sweet against tangy, crisp against chewy, sprightly against musky. It makes a nice counterpoint to any of the earthy beef dishes, and goes especially well at the end of the meal, as a palate cleanser.

Honey Mustard Dressing*

1 tablespoon fresh lemon juice
6 tablespoons olive oil
2 teaspoons mustard seeds, ground in small mortar
2 tablespoons honey
¼ teaspoon turmeric
¼ teaspoon dried dill

For every 4 salads:

mixed baby spring greens
2 cups bean sprouts, broken into halves
1 large Asian pear, quartered lengthwise
4 dried Calimyrna figs, quartered lengthwise
4 thin wedges cheese: chevre, Brie, or Parmesan

First, prepare dressing. In a small bowl, whisk lemon juice into olive oil, then add ground mustard seeds, turmeric, and dill, then honey, whisking after each addition. Set aside.

Now make composed salads. On each salad plate arrange a wreath of mixed baby spring greens, leaving a vacant space in the center of each wreath. Into the center of the wreath add ½ cup broken bean sprouts. Drizzle the bean sprouts lightly with some honey mustard dressing.

Core each Asian pear quarter, then slice lengthwise into 5 slices. Clumping these slices to resemble the uncut pear quarter, place each set of 5, skin side up, on top of the bed of bean sprouts. Snuggle a piece of quartered fig into the spaces between slices. This will make the pear slices fan out.

Drizzle more honey mustard dressing sparingly in an arc across the upper half of the fan. Add wedge of cheese as a garnish beside the lower half of the fan (optional). Refrigerate until ready to serve. Serves 4.

* There are a lot of good commercial honey mustard dressings out there. Our favorite is Larrupin's (see Resource section). But if you have nothing on hand except the raw ingredients, here is something that will work for this salad. Adjust ingredients according to your taste.

Fig and Peach in Clabbered Cream

A delicate treat for summertime, when fresh figs are available in abundance.

For each salad:

1 leaf butter lettuce
1 fresh fig, peeled and quartered lengthwise
2 tablespoons cream or half-and-half
one-half white peach, peeled and sliced lengthwise

Lay a single leaf of unbroken butter lettuce on each salad plate, like an edible green cup. Set one peeled, quartered fresh fig on this lettuce "cup," arranging the pieces seed-side up. Pour cream over fig. Refrigerate at least an hour, to allow time for the enzymes in the fig to clabber the cream.

   Just before serving, add slices of peeled white peach to encircle the fig.

Cannon Balls and Cottage Cheese

*This colorful summertime salad can be made with
cantaloupe, Sharlyn melon, honeydew, or any other
melon—or mixture of melons—that strikes your fancy.
Figure on one serving requiring half a cantaloupe.*

Per serving:

about 12 leaves baby mixed spring greens
½ cup small curd cottage cheese
10 melon balls

On each salad plate compose a wreath of spring greens.
Inside that wreath spoon a second wreath of cottage
cheese.

Now, in the center of both wreaths, build a stack of
"cannon balls," beginning with a triangle of 3 melon
balls on each side and 1 in the center. Stack 3 more
balls on top of the bottom 6. Put a single ball on top of
the whole pile.

Refrigerate until ready to serve.

I have been baking bread for almost forty years—usually two loaves a week, sometimes more. I have tried a myriad of recipes and methods and have finally settled on the two recipes contained in this book. Throughout the years, here is what I've learned:

• You don't need to waste your money on fancy designer flours, although for the novelty of it, if you ever get to an authentic stone mill such as the one we visited in Oregon [reference in Resources], you might want to try some of their flour.

• I always use the instant yeast. Haven't used the other stuff in years. This much simplifies bread-making. When using instant yeast, the water temperature is very important. It should be between 125 and 130 degrees. Use an instant-read thermometer: don't guess.

• I usually add a quarter-cup of olive oil to my bread, but this is not necessary.

• Dough thrives in a warm, moist environment. Commercial bakeries have proof ovens that maintain an 80-degree temperature and high humidity for the rising bread. The closer you can come to this ideal, the better your bread. To this end I try to work with warm mixing bowls and warm loaf pans.

• Salt is a necessity for any bread recipe, for without it, the yeast will not work.

• Sugar is not necessary; however, I like to use it because it improves the crust.

• Most bread recipes call for two risings of about 20 minutes each. I like to use a third.

• Don't over-knead the dough. Stop when it becomes a fine, smooth, silky ball.

• Punching down the bread should not be a violent act. Pull the edges of the dough toward the center and push down gently on the dough. Don't be slamming it around.

• After baking, when you think the bread is done, always take its temperature before pronouncing it done. White bread should be around 180 degrees; wheat and rye breads should be 200 to 210. Don't expect wheat or rye breads to rise as much as an all-white loaf. I like to spray water in the oven several times during the baking process. This helps to form a really nice crust. Also, it's very important to slash the tops of your loaves before putting them in the oven; otherwise, they will crack along the side and present an unattractive loaf.

Once you get the hang of bread-making, it's very easy and satisfying. At this stage, when making my standard loaf recipe, I never even think of looking at a recipe.

NOTE: For years I have experimented with sourdough bread, because it has always fascinated me, and yet to this day a loaf meeting my expectations has eluded me. Like chili, there are thousands of recipes, but I have been unable to consistently produce a good sourdough loaf. If any among you, good readers, can point me in the right direction, please do me a favor and share your insights.

All-Purpose City Bread

Bake in cast-iron loaf pans, if you're lucky enough to have them. They impart a lovely crust to these loaves. If you don't have the cast-iron models, use their ordinary cousins.

For this recipe I usually use my Kitchen-Aid mixer, but with a little more elbow-grease, the dough can easily be kneaded by hand. The result will be the same.

White City Bread:

6½ cups flour
2 tablespoons quick-rise yeast
2 tablespoons white sugar
1 teaspoon salt
2 cups water
¼ cup olive oil or canola oil

Place flour in mixer bowl. For white bread, I use Gold Medal unbleached all-purpose flour. Over the years I've experimented with many different types and brands of flour, including the expensive 4- to 5-dollar-a-pound brands. In my opinion there is absolutely no difference between those expensive designer flours and the inexpensive Gold Medal brand readily available at any supermarket.

Add yeast, sugar, and salt. I use the whisk attachment to thoroughly mix all these dry ingredients. While you are mixing, heat water (you can use your potato water here from **Parsley Potatoes,** page 53). The water must be heated to between 125 and 130 degrees. This is important when using quick-rise yeast. Use an instant-read thermometer.

To flour add water and oil (olive oil gives the better flavor). Change the whisk on the mixer to the paddle. Stir on low speed until the dough forms a shaggy mass. Scrape the paddle with a rubber spatula and form into a rough ball.

Cover mixer bowl with plastic wrap. Place towel over plastic wrap and set aside in a warm place for 15 minutes. Meanwhile, oil a medium-sized ceramic mixing bowl (use olive oil for this step) and warm it slightly in the oven. The bowl should be merely warm, not hot to the touch. Remove ceramic bowl from oven.

After the mixer bowl has sat in its warm place for 15 minutes, use a rubber spatula to coax the dough from the mixer bowl into the ceramic bowl. Move dough around in the ceramic bowl to coat it on all sides with the olive oil. Cover the ceramic bowl with the plastic wrap and towel and set aside in a warm—not hot—place. Eighty degrees is perfect.

After 20 minutes the dough should have risen to approximately double. Give it the two-finger test (stick two fingers in; if the indentations remain, the dough is ready for the next step). Turn out onto a lightly floured board. Knead for 3 to 5 minutes, forming into a smooth, satiny, round ball.

With a serrated bread knife, divide as equally as possible into two pieces. Form each piece into a ball. Invert ceramic bowl over one ball and the bowl from the mixer over the other ball. Let rest for a few minutes. Then, on a floured surface, with a rolling pin roll out each ball into an oblong a little less than an inch thick.

Now, with your fingers lift one end of the dough oblong and roll the dough, forming it into what looks like a jelly roll. Pinch the bottom to seal. Fold the ends in to the bottom and pinch to seal. Place this loaf into a warm loaf pan. (You may want to spray your loaf pans with a non-stick product, depending on how well they are seasoned.) Cover the two loaves with the plastic wrap and towel and place in warm location to let rise for 20 to 25 minutes. Meanwhile, preheat the oven to 375.

When the loaves have sufficiently risen (the two-finger test, remember?), slash the tops with a razor blade or serrated bread knife. Sprinkle lightly with flour (optional), and place in oven. After about 5 minutes or so, open the oven door and spritz in some water. This helps form a nice crust. Bake for 35 minutes. Use a timer.

After 35 minutes, pull one loaf out for testing. Plunge an instant-read thermometer into the thickest part of the loaf, avoiding the pan. For white bread, temperature should be approximately 180 degrees.

When test loaf has reached that point, remove both loaves from oven and turn out onto a cooling rack. If you want to get fancy, you can put an egg wash on them to make them look pretty. Or sometimes I just brush olive oil on.

Let rest at least 20 minutes--30 minutes is better—before slicing.

This is a very good all-around daily bread. Makes excellent sandwiches and toast and can be used for slopping up the various sauces mentioned in this book.

For variations see **Whole Wheat City Bread** and **Rye City Bread**, following.

Whole Wheat City Bread

You will notice that the whole wheat and the rye loaves do not rise as much as the white loaf. This is normal.

Follow recipe for All-Purpose City Bread, but substitute a whole wheat flour for 2 cups of the white flour in the above recipe. Bake to an internal temperature of 210 degrees, maximum.

Rye City Bread

This bread is particularly aromatic and flavorful when toasted.

Substitute rye flour for 2 cups of the white flour in recipe for White Bread. Grind 2 tablespoons of dried fennel seeds in your coffee grinder. Add these 2 ground tablespoons along with 1 tablespoon whole dried fennel seed to the recipe when mixing the dry ingredients. Also add 1 tablespoon unground caraway seeds. Bake to an internal temperature of 210 degrees.

All-Purpose Mountain Bread

This is our version of a recipe that we first saw in Issue #112 of Backwoods Home Magazine. We call it Mountain Bread because it is very easy to store and bake at our mountain cabin, once we have assembled the dry ingredients into a kit, which keeps for months or years— see beginning of method discussion.

NOTE: All ingredients must be weighed on your digital scale.
2nd NOTE: *This recipe takes 24 hours.*

White Mountain Bread

15 ounces unbleached all-purpose white flour
1½ teaspoons salt
1 tablespoon powdered confectioner's sugar
¼ teaspoon instant yeast
10½ ounces tepid water
1 egg white (optional)

Essential Equipment

#8 cast iron skillet with lid
plastic wrap
clean side rag or tea towel
cooking oil spray (Pam or equivalent)
instant-read thermometer
parchment paper

Assemble all DRY ingredients and mix well with a wire whisk. At this point you have your bread kit. We usually make 5 or 6 of these bread kits at a time, vacuum sealing each kit, and take them to the cabin.

The day before baking, mix dry ingredients with 10½ ounces of tepid water (warm to the touch, but not boiling). Mix with wooden spoon. This will form a very sticky, shaggy dough. Don't add any more water or any more flour. Work into a ball as best you can, in the bowl. Cover bowl with plastic wrap, put a clean, dry cloth over the plastic wrap, and set aside in a warm place for 18 to 24 hours, the longer the better.

Two hours before baking, punch down dough, take out of bowl, and on a lightly floured surface form into a ball and knead for 1 to 2 minutes. It will still be sticky. Resist the temptation to add a lot more flour; you don't need it.

Wash and dry the bowl. Cut about a 12x18" rectangle of parchment paper. Place paper in bowl; place dough on top of the paper. Spray top of dough ball with cooking oil (Pam or equivalent). Cover bowl again with plastic wrap (use the same piece) and cloth. Set aside.

Approximately ½ hour before baking, place a covered cast iron skillet (#8 works well) in the oven. Bring oven to 500 degrees. After 30 minutes, remove skillet—CAREFULLY, it will be very hot!—reduce oven temperature to 425 degrees, and place dough ball (on parchment paper) into skillet. Slash top of dough ball with a razor blade or serrated bread knife. Put the lid on, put covered skillet back in oven for 30 minutes. After 30 minutes, uncover, spritz some water into the oven to raise some steam. This will help form a nice crust.

Close oven and bake, uncovered, for 5 more minutes. Check temperature with instant-read thermometer. For white bread the temperature should be at least 180. When bread is at that point, pull it out, remove from skillet, remove paper, place on cooling rack. Let it cool for at least 20 minutes before slicing. If you want to pretty it up, you can put an egg wash on it: ½ teaspoon cold water, white of one egg, whisked together with a pastry brush.

Important, Tasty, Simple Variations:

Whole Wheat Mountain Bread

Replace 6 ounces of the white flour with whole wheat flour. Bake until temperature reaches 210 degrees.

Rye Mountain Bread

Replace 6 ounces of the white flour with a dark rye flour. Grind 1 tablespoon caraway seed and 1 tablespoon fennel seed in a coffee grinder. (Don't bother cleaning coffee grinder before or grinding, since the coffee adds a very slight flavoring to the bread, and next morning when you grind your beans, you'll find that your coffee has a very interesting hint of spices.) Add to dry ingredients, plus ½ teaspoon each of the whole seeds. Bake until temperature reaches 210 degrees.

Corn Bread in Cast Iron

A lot of people like to put jalapeño in cornbread. I could never understand this, but if you want to, then do so. I like crumpled bacon or **Chicken Cracklings** *(stolen from your dog treats, page 157) added to the ingredients before baking.*

1 cup yellow or white cornmeal or combination
1 cup unbleached all-purpose white flour
3 tablespoons sugar
1 tablespoon baking powder
1 teaspoon salt
⅓ cup olive or canola oil
1 egg
1 cup milk
1 tablespoon chicken fat (or bacon fat or canola oil)

Combine dry ingredients in medium-sized mixing bowl. Mix well. In small mixing bowl combine wet ingredients: oil, egg, and milk. Mix well. Add milk mixture to the dry ingredients and stir until just blended.

Into an 8" iron skillet put chicken fat. Warm the skillet to melt the chicken fat. Swirl to completely coat bottom and sides of the skillet; pour off any excess.

Pour corn bread ingredients into skillet, starting at the center of the skillet and letting the ingredients push the chicken fat to the edges.

Bake in preheated 400-degree oven for 25 minutes or until a toothpick comes out clean. Let cool on baking rack for 10 minutes. Cut in wedges and serve in skillet or turn out onto baking rack and serve however it pleases you. Serves 6 to 8.

Quick, Easy, and Very Good Garlic Bread

For a crowd:

1 loaf high-quality sourdough bread*

Slice the loaf diagonally at ¾ inch intervals but don't slice all the way through. Drizzle olive oil in the slits. Throw in some garlic seasoning (we use Johnny's Garlic Seasoning from Costco—remember, this is quick-and-dirty) and some off-the-shelf Italian seasonings and grated Parmesan cheese. Wrap tightly in foil. Put in 300-degree oven until your dinner is ready.

For 3 or 4:

Cut off 3 to 4 large slices and follow the same procedure as above. Wrap in foil, cook at 350 degrees for half an hour or so. Remove from oven, open foil, and place under a heated broiler. Watch it closely and when it starts to smoke, pull it out and throw on a little more cheese. The bread will be crusty and bubbly.

Skillet Biscuits

For the solid shortening, what really works great, if you're lucky enough to have it, is bear fat. Butter will work, too.

1 teaspoon salt
1 tablespoon baking powder
1¾ cups all-purpose white flour
½ cup solid shortening
1 cup water OR
1 cup milk

Mix dry ingredients thoroughly. Cut in shortening. Gradually stir in water or milk to form a stiff, shaggy dough.

Turn out onto floured surface and briefly knead (no more than a minute). Roll out with floured rolling pin to form an oval about ½ to ¾-inch thick. Using a 3" biscuit cutter, cut out as many biscuits as you can— probably 10 to 12.

Place on large, well-seasoned, cast-iron skillet. Place ½-inch apart if you like your biscuits with crust on all sides, or place close together if you only want the crust on top. For a brown finish, brush the tops with milk, melted butter, or olive oil.

Bake in preheated oven at 450 degrees for 12 to 15 minutes, depending on thickness. Makes 10 to 12.

Variation:

For extra-crusty biscuits, spritz some water into the oven about 5 or 6 minutes into the baking process.

You don't associate desserts with cast iron? You're in for a surprise.

A good old #8 skillet can handle everything from the plebian
(a deep-dish **Mountain Apple Pie**)
to the patrician (**Stanford Cheesecake**)
and a lot of confection territory in between.

You've never seen chocolate cake in a corn-stick pan?
Check out **Chocolate Pine Cones** for a change of pace.
And cast iron bread loaf pans are perfect for **Pan de Tres Leches.**

I wouldn't worry too much about appearances.
There's something flagrantly self-assured about bringing cheesecake to the table
in a cast-iron skillet.

"That's the way we do it around here," I always tell 'em.
But if you *must* serve on fine china, just make up the portions in the kitchen.
Except for the flavor, they'll never know.

135

Stanford Cheesecake

This is the cheesecake that made friends angle for an invitation to Lagunita's Sunday night dinners, back in my Stanford undergraduate days. This is the cheesecake whose secret I tried to wangle out of the dining hall's nutritionist. "I won't give you the recipe," she said, "but I'll let you work to earn it." So I traded some typing for the institutional-sized recipe, whose quantities I scaled down for the home kitchen.

This cheesecake has been a favorite of my dinner guests for two generations or more. Believe it or not, you can make it in a cast-iron skillet as well as in a fluted glass pie dish. And it's even tastier the next day.

Crust
14 graham crackers
2 tablespoons sugar
¼ cup butter

Filling
2 eggs
½ cup sugar

12 ounces cream cheese, softened
1 teaspoon vanilla
½ teaspoon milk

Topping
1 pint sour cream
3 tablespoons sugar
½ teaspoon vanilla

Place graham crackers in a Zip-loc bag and roll with a rolling pin until you have a bag of fine crumbs. Add sugar and shake to mix well. Melt butter in a small skillet. Add sugared crumbs and stir with a fork until well blended. Pour into a lightly buttered cast iron skillet or fluted glass pie plate. Shape into a crust of consistent thickness on the sides as well as the bottom of your container. Set aside.

In a small mixing bowl, beat eggs until light and fluffy. Continue beating as you add sugar, a little at a time. Now beat in the softened cream cheese a little at a time. After each addition of cream cheese, beat until no lumps remain. When all the cream cheese has been accommodated, add vanilla and milk and stir thoroughly. Pour filling over graham cracker pie crust, smoothing with a rubber spatula.

Bake in preheated 375-degree oven for 10 to 15 minutes, or until filling is custardy (not runny) but crust has not gotten burned. Remove from oven and set aside to cool for 10 minutes, during which time turn oven down to 350 degrees and hold there.

While cheesecake is cooling, make topping. In the small mixing bowl, stir sour cream together with sugar and vanilla until well mixed. After cheesecake has cooled for 10 minutes, pour topping over and smooth with rubber spatula.

Return to oven at 350 degrees for 5 minutes. Remove from oven and set aside to cool, then refrigerate until ready to serve. Serves 12.

Strawberried Rummed Pound Cake

An easy, fast, and distinctive flavor riff on the time-honored strawberry shortcake.

For each two desserts:

2 one-inch slices frozen butter pound cake
8 large, ripe strawberries, sliced
½ cup light sour cream
1 teaspoon vanilla extract
1 tablespoon powdered sugar
¼ cup rum in which dried strawberries have soaked (held over from Strawberry Macadamia Cookies)

For each dessert, place sliced pound cake in serving dish. Cover with 4 sliced strawberries. In a small bowl, mix sour cream, vanilla, and powdered sugar. Spread over strawberries. Drizzle strawberry-flavored rum over all. Set aside in the refrigerator for half an hour before serving, to allow the rum to penetrate down to the pound cake. Serves 2.

And speaking of held-over soaking liquors (such as the rum from **Cherry Chews** [p. 48] and the crème de menthe from **Chocolate Mint Surprise** cookies [p. 49], and the crème de cacao from **Chocolate Pine Cones** [p. 141]), here's your chance to come up with some pound cake twists of your own.

I can picture a slice of pound cake, a scoop of chocolate ice cream, and the held-over crème de menthe or crème de cacao drizzled over all and topped with toasted slivered almonds or Hershey chocolate syrup.   Or **Easy Chocolate Glaze** (p. 142).

What do you envision?

Pan de Tres Leches (Three-Milk Cake)

When I was teaching English as a Second Language, my Mexican students would occasionally declare a class holiday—Mother's Day, always, and teacher's birthday, certainly. At the class break, they would all excuse themselves for a moment; when they marched proudly back in, bearing a full-fledged potluck feast, teacher just **had** *to honor their efforts.*

On one such unforgettable impromptu fiesta, I first encountered and promptly fell in love with this "postre" . . . dessert. There are many variations on this basic theme—a substantial cake soaked in a milky bath—but this is my spin [in brackets] on the way an obliging student wrote it down for me that day. In Spanish.

Cake
3 eggs
1 cup sugar [turbinado preferred]
1 teaspoon vanilla
1¼ cup [unbleached all-purpose] flour
2 teaspoons baking powder

Filling
1 cup evaporated milk (save surplus*)
1 cup sweetened condensed milk (save surplus*)
1 can Nestle's media crema**

Beat eggs until light. Continue beating as you add sugar a little at a time. Add vanilla; beat until foamy.

Mix flour with baking powder. Add to the wet mixture. Beat for about a minute.

Turn into two ungreased loaf pans and bake in a preheated 400-degree oven for 20 minutes, or until a toothpick comes out clean. Remove pans from oven and set aside to cool.

Mix the evaporated and condensed milks with the media crema until all is mixed well. Use the blender if necessary. Let stand until at room temperature. (Save back surplus

When cake in loaf pans is cool, prick surface with a fork. Do this carefully to prevent the cake's breaking apart. Pour the 3-milks mixture slowly over the cakes, a little at a time, until all is absorbed. [Be patient. The cake will need time to absorb the milky mixture. You'll see it "burping" as air rises up through the fork-holes. It may appear as if all that liquid will never fit in the loaf pan, but if you give it time, it will all soak in.]

Refrigerate at least one hour before serving [to give the milks mixture a chance to set up]. [Refrigerating overnight is even better.] Top with whipped cream if you really want to go overboard. Fills 2 standard-size bread loaf pans. Each pan serves 6.

Especially good after a spicy dinner. ¡Muy rico!

*   Cans of evaporated milk and sweetened condensed milk each contain more than 1 cup of liquid. Save back surplus to make French toast:

French Toast Dos Leches

Combine milks, add 2 beaten eggs, beat till blended. Dip dry bread slices in mixture, then in a cast iron skillet or on a griddle over medium heat, fry each slice in 1 teaspoon butter. Turn once, adding more butter as necessary.

** Available at Mexican food sections of supermarkets.

Peach Paradox

If you can't decide between pudding and cake but like the flavors of cheesecake and of peaches, try this dish. It eats like a light cake on the top, but inside, it resembles spiced peaches topped with a cheesecake-flavored pudding.

Here's what a fan had to say about this recipe:

"I doubled this recipe and cooked it in a dutch oven while out camping this past weekend. It was a wonderful success and I became the dutch oven expert that night. The peaches were fresh off my sister's tree, and, well, it was one of the best desserts I have had in a long time. This recipe has become a keeper in my growing dutch oven recipe file."
—Quietgentleman (from www.backwoodshome.com/forum)

½ cup brown sugar
½ teaspoon cinnamon
1¼ cup flour
2 tablespoons butter, softened
2 fresh peaches
2 eggs
¼ cup white sugar
1 cup light sour cream
2 teaspoons baking powder

In a small bowl sift brown sugar, cinnamon, and ¼ cup of the flour. Cut in softened butter until mixture is crumbly and pea-sized. Distribute this mixture into two portions. Spread one of these portions evenly across the bottom of a 7" wide, 1¾ quart casserole.

Slice two fresh peaches and distribute slices on top of the butter/sugar mixture.

Beat 2 eggs until light and fluffy. Beat in white sugar, then add sour cream and beat entire mixture until light, fluffy, and free of lumps.

Sift reserved 1 cup flour with the baking powder. Add to the moist mixture and again, beat until free of lumps.

Pour batter over peaches, then sprinkle reserved butter/sugar mixture on top of the batter.

Bake at 375° for 40 minutes or until a toothpick inserted into the middle of the cake topping comes out clean.

Serves 4-6.

Chocolate Pine Cones

1 cup jicama, minced
crème de cacao to cover, about ½ cup
3 eggs
¾ cup sugar (turbinado preferred)
2 tablespoons Hershey chocolate syrup
¼ cup Dutch baker's chocolate (cocoa)
1¼ cup flour
2 teaspoons baking powder
¼ cup pine nuts

Place minced jicama in a small mug; pour crème de cacao over. Set aside for at least an hour for color and flavor to absorb into the jicama. Then drain jicama, reserving crème de cacao for another use.

Beat eggs until light and fluffy. Beat in sugar and chocolate syrup; beat for at least a minute. Add Dutch baker's chocolate, stir to mix well, beat again. Add marinated, drained jicama. Mix well.

Sift flour with baking powder. Add to mixing bowl; stir thoroughly. Add pine nuts, stir again until all is well mixed.

Pour batter into 2 lightly buttered cast iron corn-stick pans, or into 1 cast iron corn-stick pan and 1 lightly buttered cast iron loaf pan, or if you don't have corn-stick pans, pour into 2 lightly buttered cast iron loaf pans or other loaf pans. Bake in preheated 400-degree oven for 18–20 minutes or until a toothpick comes out clean. Turn out on racks to cool. Makes 14 "corn-stick" shapes—we're calling them pine cones—or about 16 (2" wide) servings from loaf pans.

Top with **Easy Chocolate Glaze** (see next page).

Serve glazed "pine cones" alongside vanilla ice cream or vanilla-flavored frozen yogurt. Or serve as a moist version of biscotti, to dip in coffee or espresso.

Easy Chocolate Glaze

*Use this on **Chocolate Pine Cones** or Pine Cone Bars (page 141)*

4 tablespoons butter, melted
2 tablespoons Dutch baker's chocolate
4 teaspoons agave nectar (or corn syrup)

In a #3 (6½" cast iron skillet, melt the butter. To melted butter add Dutch baker's chocolate, stirring to blend thoroughly. Add agave nectar and again stir thoroughly.

While mixture is still warm, pour over Chocolate Pine Cones a little at a time. Wait for the air holes in the pine cones to absorb the mixture, then repeat.

You can speed the firming-up process by refrigerating the glazed pine cones.

Linda's Mountain Apple Pie

First, you got your basic, healthful, olive oil pie crust:

3 cups unbleached all-purpose flour
1½ teaspoons sea salt
½ cup extra virgin olive oil
2 tablespoons butter
½ cup cold water

Sift flour with sea salt. Mix in olive oil and butter, cut in small chunks. Mix with fingers until you have little lumps the size of small peas. Add cold water, a little at a time, until dough holds together. Divide into two balls. Roll out thin and ease the bottom crust into a well-seasoned, ungreased, 8-inch cast iron skillet.

Next, you got your filling:

5 or 6 medium-sized Granny Smith apples
½ cup turbinado or dark brown sugar
2 tablespoons flour
1-2 teaspoons cinnamon

Peel and core apples. Cut in slivers and lay evenly on the bottom crust. Over that sprinkle sugar mixed with flour and cinnamon. Don't make it too sweet at this stage.

Now it gets creative. Take your pick:

½ cup or a big fistful of some kind of chopped nuts (walnuts, pecans, pick your favorite. Pine nuts are good, too)
⅓ cup or a small fistful of some kind of dried fruit (cranberries, cherries, raisins, whatever the kids haven't eaten)

Can't do without:

¼ cup dark rum sprinkled over the whole mess
2-3 tablespoons molasses

Sprinkle rum over all pie ingredients. Drizzle molasses over everything in a spiral with about 1-inch intervals.

Put on the top crust. Don't worry if it falls apart; just make it into little shingles and tell folks that's the way we do it around here. Eats the same.

Bake it:

Start at 450 degrees for about, oh, 25 minutes if you're at any altitude, less if you're at sea level. Then kick it down to about 350 degrees and continue to bake until it

Looks like pie, nice and brown;
Smells like pie, emitting heavenly aromas; and
Sounds like pie, making little sizzles around the edges.

Remove from oven, let it cool 15 to 20 minutes on a rack, cut it up, pass it around, take the compliments with a smile, and tell 'em I taught you how.

Limón Colada #1

This recipe uses only one mixing bowl and one small cast iron skillet.

2 tablespoons butter
12 vanilla wafers
¼ cup sliced almonds
½ cup sweetened baking coconut
1 egg
½ cup sweetened condensed milk
1 medium-sized lemon or lime
2 ripe kiwis

In a #3, (6½") cast iron skillet, melt butter over very low heat. When melted, set aside to cool. Meanwhile, put vanilla wafers in a small Zip-loc bag and roll with a rolling pin until they are fine crumbs. In a small mixing bowl, chop slivered almonds. Add vanilla wafer crumbs and coconut to the chopped almonds. Mix well. Pour melted butter over this mixture and stir with a fork to distribute butter evenly. Spoon mixture into skillet and pat it gently over bottom and sides, as you would a graham cracker crust. Set skillet aside.

Now, in the same bowl you used for the crumb mixture, beat egg until light and fluffy. Continue beating as you add condensed milk. Grate the rind of the lemon or lime and add to the egg and milk mixture, stirring to blend. Slice the lime or lemon in half and extract the juice (you can do this with an old-fashioned juicing tool suspended over the mixing bowl). Blend juice into egg and milk mixture. Beat by hand for two minutes; the mixture will begin to coddle and become custard-like.

Pour custardy mixture into skillet. Now, in the same bowl, slice kiwi very thin. Set aside while you bake the custardy mixture.

Bake skillet in preheated 425 degree oven for 13 minutes or until crust is brown and custard has set. Remove from oven and cool 10 minutes. Carefully arrange kiwi slices over the top of the custard, making two layers if necessary.

Cool another half hour, then refrigerate for 2 hours. Before serving, top with whipped cream if desired. Slice and serve cold. Serves 4.

Limón Colada #2

This tastes like key lime on the bottom, cheesecake on top.

6 tablespoons butter
30 vanilla wafers
½ cup sliced almonds
1 cup sweetened baking coconut
2 eggs
1 cup sweetened condensed milk
zest and juice of 2 limes
1 pint light sour cream
5 heaping tablespoons powdered sugar
1 tablespoon dark rum
2 ripe kiwis

In a small skillet, melt butter over very low heat. When melted, set aside to cool. Meanwhile, put vanilla wafers in a small Zip-loc bag and roll with a rolling pin until they are fine crumbs. In a small mixing bowl, chop slivered almonds. Add coconut and chopped almonds to the Zip-loc bag with the vanilla wafer crumbs. Mix well. Pour this mixture into the skillet with the melted butter and stir with a fork to distribute butter evenly. Spoon mixture into pie plate and pat it gently over bottom and sides, as you would a graham cracker crust. Set aside.

Beat eggs until light and fluffy. Continue beating as you add condensed milk. Grate the rind of the lime and add to the egg and milk mixture, stirring to blend. Slice the lime or lemon in half and extract the juice (you can do this with an old-fashioned juicing tool suspended over the mixing bowl). Blend juice into egg and milk mixture. Beat by hand for two minutes; the mixture will begin to coddle and become custard-like.

Pour custardy mixture into pie plate. Bake in preheated 425 degree oven for 13 minutes or until crust is brown and custard has set. Remove from oven and cool 10 minutes. Lower heat in oven to 350 degrees.

Meanwhile, in a small bowl beat sour cream; stir in sugar and then stir in rum.

Pour over custard layer. Return to 350 degree oven for 5 minutes. Remove, cool on rack, then refrigerate for 2 hours. Top with slices of kiwi, refrigerate another hour. Serve cold. Serves 8 to 12.

Not-Your-Mother's Pumpkin Pie

The only ingredients this pie has in common with its traditional cousin are eggs, pumpkin, and cinnamon. Flavorwise, it has more in common with pumpkin cheesecake, though it's decidedly lower in fat.

16 graham crackers
1 cup chopped pecans, whirled in coffee grinder
8 tablespoons melted butter
2 eggs, beaten
1 cup light sour cream
2 cups canned pumpkin
1 teaspoon cinnamon
1 teaspoon candied ginger, whirled in coffee grinder
2 tablespoons butterscotch ice cream topping
pecan halves

Roll crackers or cookies into fine crumbs (a Zip-loc bag is helpful for this). Melt butter in small skillet. Add crumbs and toss with a fork until butter is well distributed. Put buttered crumbs into an 8½-inch iron skillet and pat to form a pie crust. Set aside.

In a medium-sized bowl, beat eggs until light; add sour cream, pumpkin, seasonings, and butterscotch ice cream topping. Stir until well blended. Pour into skillet containing the pie crust. Arrange pecan halves on top.

Bake at 350 degrees for 45 minutes. Serves about 8.

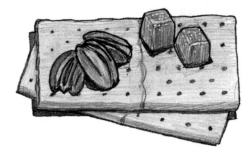

146

Tropicana Treat

Moist, tangy, light, and flavorful, this miniature pie complements roasts, chops, and fish. It performs well as a company dessert. Vanilla flavored frozen yogurt would make a good accompaniment.

6 tablespoons butter, divided
4 tablespoons olive oil
1 egg, beaten
1 banana, mashed with a fork
1 ripe mango, chopped fine
juice of ½ medium-sized lime
¼ cup candied ginger, chopped fine
1 cup flour
1 teaspoon baking powder
2 tablespoons turbinado sugar
2 tablespoons dark brown sugar
¼ cup slivered almonds, chopped fine
¼ cup sweetened baker's coconut

Cream 4 tablespoons of the butter; drizzle in olive oil and beat until well blended. Add egg, beat until blended. Add mashed banana and chopped mango. Add lime juice and chopped ginger. Beat all until well blended.

In separate bowl, sift flour and baking powder, add turbinado sugar and dark brown sugar; mix together.

Combine wet and dry ingredients, mixing well. Turn into buttered (#5, 8") iron skillet.

In a small (#3, 6½") skillet, over low heat melt remaining 2 tablespoons butter. Remove skillet from heat; add almonds and coconut and stir until well blended. Sprinkle mixture over batter in the 8" skillet.

Bake at 350 degrees for 35 minutes or until coconut is browned and a toothpick inserted in the center comes out clean. Cool on rack. Top with whipped cream if desired, or serve accompanied by a small scoop of vanilla flavored frozen yogurt. Serves 6 to 8.

Sour Cream Shortcake with Summer Fruit

Light and delicious, this shortcake tastes rather like a moist and fluffy scone. Served with fresh fruits and a topping of light sour cream, it makes a refreshing summer lunch all by itself.

Shortcake
1 cup unbleached all-purpose flour
3 tablespoons turbinado sugar
2 teaspoons baking powder
4 tablespoons butter
½ cup light sour cream

In a medium-sized bowl, mix flour, sugar, and baking powder. Cut in butter, then cut in sour cream. Form into loosely packed ball, turn out on floured board, and knead a few strokes. Roll lightly, keeping dough at least an inch thick. Cut into circles with doughnut cutter or cup measure. Place in an ungreased #5 (8-inch) cast iron skillet. Bake in preheated 450° oven 18 minutes. Remove from oven and serve warm. Makes 4 shortcake biscuits (about 3" diameter).

To serve, slice circles in half crosswise. Place two shortcake halves on each plate and top with spoonfuls of fruit mixture of your choice (see suggestions below). Top all with dollops of topping mixture.

Fruit Mixture
In a medium-sized serving bowl, toss together any combination of the following, or any other summer fruits or nuts of your choice.
½ cup fresh blueberries
1 white peach, peeled and cut in small chunks
½ cup Bing or Queen Anne cherries, pitted and cut in chunks
½ cup fresh strawberries, sliced
1 banana, peeled and sliced crosswise
4–6 dice of candied ginger, slivered or cut fine
½ cup walnut pieces

Topping Mixture
½ cup light sour cream
2 tablespoons turbinado sugar
½ teaspoon vanilla extract
Mix all together and serve in a small bowl to ladle over fruit and shortcake.

Cast Iron Cuisine

Apple Love Pats

Think apple-flavored coffee cake.

½ medium apple, tart or sweet, chopped fine
2 tablespoons water
2 tablespoons turbinado sugar
½ teaspoon concentrated lemon juice*
*if apple is of a sweet variety (omit for tangy apples)
2 tablespoons butter
2 tablespoons macadamia nuts, sliced and chopped
1 egg, beaten
1 teaspoon lemon extract
½ cup unbleached all-purpose flour
¼ cup nonfat dried milk
1 teaspoon baking powder
1–2 tablespoons evaporated milk (if necessary)

In a small saucepan, combine finely chopped apple, water, and sugar, adding lemon juice if you're working with a sweet apple. Over a low heat, cook the mixture, alternately mashing with a potato ricer and stirring as the mixture cooks down. Continue until water has evaporated and you're left with a small amount of what looks like a syrupy brown applesauce. Set aside to cool.

In a #3 cast iron skillet, melt butter. Swirl to coat sides of skillet. Add macadamia nuts and stir to coat with butter. Remove nuts and set aside. Let butter cool, then in a small mixing bowl, add to beaten egg. Add lemon extract and cooled apple mixture. Stir to mix thoroughly.

Combine flour with dried milk and baking powder. Add to wet mixture. Stir to mix thoroughly. Batter should be wet and shaggy. If it seems too dry, add 1 to 2 tablespoons evaporated milk and mix well.

Turn into #3 cast iron skillet and top with buttered macadamia nuts, pressing nuts slightly into batter and easing batter to edges of the skillet.

Bake in preheated 375° oven for 15 minutes, or until lightly browned and a toothpick comes out clean. Remove from oven and let cool on rack. Cut into wedges and serve with a thin sliver of Cheddar cheese or top with whipping cream. Serves 2–4.

Strawberry Snacking Cake

The acidic strawberries interact with the sour cream to enhance the rising action of the baking powder, making this a light and porous tea cake. We prefer our cakes and cookies on the only-slightly-sweet side. If you like a sweeter confection, add 2 more tablespoons turbinado to the strawberry pulp and double the amount of sugar in the cheese spread.

1 pound large fresh strawberries
2 tablespoons turbinado sugar
2 eggs
¼ cup light sour cream
1 teaspoon lemon extract
1½ cups unbleached all-purpose flour
2 teaspoons baking powder
¼ cup dried nonfat milk
2 tablespoons butter
3 tablespoons sliced almonds
½ cup Neufchatel cheese
2 tablespoons powdered sugar
or 1 tablespoon agave nectar

Set aside 3 large strawberries. In a blender, whirl (at chop speed) 6 large strawberries or a number sufficient to produce ¾ cup strawberry pulp. Don't completely liquefy this; you want some small chunks to remain. Place strawberry pulp in small mixing bowl and add sugar, then beat until sugar has dissolved. Set aside.

Beat eggs until light and fluffy. Add sour cream and lemon extract; beat to blend. Add sweetened strawberry pulp. Blend well.

Mix flour, dried milk, and baking powder. Add to wet ingredients. Beat to blend thoroughly. Turn batter into a buttered cast iron loaf pan, smoothing out batter to edges of pan.

Melt butter in small (#3) cast iron skillet. Turn off heat. Add almonds to skillet and stir to moisten nuts with the melted butter. Sprinkle buttered almonds and any remaining butter over the top of the batter in the loaf pan.

Bake in preheated 375 degree oven 20 minutes or until top is golden brown and a toothpick inserted in the center comes out clean. Remove from oven and place loaf pan on a rack to cool.

Meanwhile, soften Neufchatel cheese and beat in powdered sugar or agave nectar. Chop the 3 reserved strawberries into small pieces and work them into the cheese. When tea cake has cooled to lukewarm, slice and serve with this mixture as a spread. Serves 6 to 8.

Jicama Tea Cake

Slightly crunchy, light and flavorful, this tea cake is adaptable to a number of different flavor directions.

1 cup minced jicama, divided
2 tablespoons butter
2 eggs
4 tablespoons sweetened condensed milk
2 teaspoons anise extract
¾ cup unbleached all-purpose flour
2 teaspoons baking powder

Melt butter in a #5 skillet. Swirl to cover sides. Add ¼ cup minced jicama and cook, stirring, over low flame until jicama bits become golden brown. Take off flame and set aside to cool.

Beat eggs until light and fluffy. Add sweetened concdensed milk and beat to blend. Add anise extract, stir to blend.

Using a sieve, drain melted butter into egg mixture. Save browned jicama bits and set aside. Add reserved ¾ cup uncooked jicama bits to mixture and beat to blend all ingredients thoroughly.

Mix flour and baking powder together. Add wet ingredients to dry. Mix thoroughly. Turn batter into the same #5 skillet you melted butter in. Sprinkle browned, buttered jicama bits over the top.

Bake in preheated 375° oven for 20 minutes or until a toothpick comes out clean. Remove from oven and serve slices while still warm. Serves 6 to 8.

Variations:

Substitute orange extract for anise and add 1 teaspoon ground cardamom.

Or substitute lemon extract for anise and add 2 teaspoons lemon zest.

Fudge Pie with Peanut Butter Crust

Crust
2 cups unbleached all-purpose flour
1 teaspoon sea salt
1 teaspoon cinnamon
4 tablespoons butter
10 tablespoons creamy peanut butter
12 tablespoons ice water

Mix flour, salt, and cinnamon. Cut in butter and peanut butter. Sprinkle ice water over and mix in with fork. Divide into two balls, place each ball between two sheets of waxed paper, and roll out thin. Peel off top sheet of waxed paper, invert and ease bottom crust into #5 skillet, then peel off remaining waxed paper.

Set aside top crust and skillet containing bottom crust while you prepare the filling.

Filling
8 tablespoons butter (one stick)
2 entire (8-wedge) tablets Mexican chocolate
4 tablespoons dark brown sugar
4 teaspoons vanilla
½ cup evaporated milk
1 egg, beaten
1 cup flour
1 cup chopped walnuts

In a #3 cast iron skillet, melt butter and chocolate over lowest possible flame, stirring gently with a wooden spoon to mix.

Remove from stove and transfer melted mixture to a medium-sized mixing bowl. Add brown sugar and vanilla; stir to blend. Stir in evaporated milk and beaten egg a little at a time, then gradually add flour and blend well. Add walnuts and stir thoroughly.

Add filling to skillet, spreaing out evenly. Add top crust. Fold edges of bottom crust over top crust and crimp to seal.

Bake in preheated 450° oven for 20 minutes or until crust is lightly browned. Remove skillet from oven and cool on rack. When thoroughly cool, cut in thin slices and serve. Top with whipped cream if desired (not necessary—this dish is plenty rich as it is). Serves 8–10.

Wee Lemon Pie

Very easy to make, this treat is as tangy as key lime pie, but with a chewy/crunchy crust.

¾ cup chopped walnuts
¾ cup sweetened baker's coconut
4 tablespoons butter
2 eggs
6 tablespoons sweetened condensed milk
zest and juice of one medium lemon (about 3
**   tablespoons juice)**

Shake chopped walnuts and coconut in a plastic bag to mix. In a #3 cast iron skillet, melt butter. Add walnut/coconut mixture and stir to coat with melted butter, then pat to thinly but evenly cover bottom and sides of skillet.

Beat eggs until light and fluffy. Add sweetened condensed milk a little at a time, stirring to mix. Add lemon zest and lemon juice a little at a time, stirring to mix.

Pour into skillet. Bake in preheated 375° oven 20 minutes, until custard is set and coconut is lightly browned. Remove from oven and set aside to cool, then refrigerate for an hour before serving. Serves 4.

Wood Stove Baked Apple or Poached Pear for Two

You can, of course, cook this on your stove top rather than your wood stove, if you prefer. Adjust proportions if you want to serve more than two diners.

1 large apple, Macintosh, Rome, or similar
2 tablespoons rum
½ teaspoon molasses
2 teaspoons raw sugar
1 tablespoon creamy peanut butter
2–3 cubes candied ginger, minced fine
1 graham cracker, crumbled fine

Cut apple in half horizontally and core. Place in casserole or in cast iron skillet cut side up. Pour rum over apple. Drizzle molasses over apple halves. Sprinkle with sugar. Cover with aluminum foil or the skillet lid and place on moderate-heat wood stove for about an hour.

While apples are cooking on wood stove, blend peanut butter with minced candied ginger and graham cracker crumbs. Reserve for topping.

When ready to serve, spoon apple halves into small bowls and pour reduced rum over. Top each baked apple half with a dollop of peanut butter mixture.
Serve hot. Serves 2.
If desired, top with whipped cream or vanilla-flavored yogurt, but this is almost gilding the lily, for this dessert is perfect as it stands.

Variation:

Wood Stove Poached Pear

Use a Bosc pear, split lengthwise and cored. Omit molasses drizzle and sugar sprinkle, but use the same amount of rum.
Cook on stove top same as apple. Serve warm, garnished with 2 tablespoons Neufachtel cheese, creamed with 2–3 minced cubes candied ginger and one tablespoon finely chopped walnuts. Different flavor, same great hot dessert.

*W*hen we're baking or cooking, let's not forget our furry friends.
There's something satisfying about baking a doggie treat yourself,
rather than bringing home store-bought dog biscuits.

Besides, this is a wonderful opportunity to use those excess fats
you've cut away or drained from your meats: bacon drippings, chicken fat, meat fat—
all are wholesome ingredients that can nourish your pets.

And if you're unsure of your ability to invent a baked product, consider this:
your dog is going to be far less critical of the finished product than your spouse might be.
So go ahead and give your imagination full rein.

There are two basic strategies for turning scraps and staples into tasty dog treats.
Consider that you're either making a pie dough or else you're baking biscuits or a cake.
For dry, hard, traditional "dog biscuits," bake in a slow oven for a long time.
Biscuits such as you'd eat yourself, go in the oven hot and fast.
"Cakes" are somewhere in the middle.
Now go out and create something.

"Lucky Dog" Treats

This is a good way to use those fat scraps you've trimmed from your raw meat and saved. Beef brisket fat is particularly easy to work with. It produces a savory-smelling treat that seems coarse to a human's taste, but that your lucky dog will drool over.

3 cups flour (whole wheat, spelt, or unbleached
   white or a combination thereof)
2 teaspoons sea salt
¾ cup solid animal fat (chicken, beef, whatever)
   cut as fine as you can get it
¼ cup fat drippings (chicken, beef, whatever),
   warmed to a liquid state if necessary
2 eggs, beaten
10 tablespoons stock or canned consommé

Assemble this recipe as you would a pie dough. Sift flour with salt, then cut in finely minced solid animal fat until you have pea-sized pieces. Add liquid fat drippings and the beaten eggs, stirring until well blended. Add (cool) stock as you would add water to pie dough, stirring all until well blended. You want a nice stiff dough, neither sticky nor rock-hard.

Turn out on a lightly floured board. Knead about one minute, then roll into a slab ½" thick. Using a doughnut cutter with the center removed, cut out circles of dough. Slice each circle into quarters as you would a pie. Trim away any overhanging morsels of solid fat. If you have spaced your circles close together, you will find that the pieces between circles will resemble small bones. Shape these pieces with your fingers to enhance the "bone" effect. Place pieces on ungreased cookie sheet.

Bake in preheated 450 degree oven for 15 minutes, during which time the treats will begin to sizzle and will shrink slightly. Turn oven down to about 250 and continue baking for 45 minutes more. Remove from oven, turn each treat upside down so the top can absorb the melted fats remaining on the pan, then set aside to cool.

Makes 68.

Cheesey Chucks

You could eat these yourself, if you were so inclined, but your pup will thank you for his share.

1 cup cornmeal
2 cups unbleached all purpose flour
2 teaspoons baking powder
2 tablespoons garlic powder
½ pound sharp Cheddar cheese, grated
1 egg, beaten
12 tablespoons milk

In a mixing bowl, sift together cornmeal, flour, baking powder, and garlic powder. Grate Cheddar cheese over the flour mixture and mix thoroughly. Your fingers will do fine for this task. Add the beaten egg and the milk; stir to mix well. Turn out onto a floured board and knead for a minute or two. Roll out dough to about ¼" thick. Use a biscuit cutter to cut circles, then slice each circle into quarters. Place on ungreased baking sheet. Bake in a preheated 300 degree oven for 1 hour. Makes 68.

Chicken Cracklings

*Often when Matt finds whole chickens on sale, usually put up two to a bag, he buys them. He uses one that evening for **Birds in Iron** (page 94) and the other he cuts up for the freezer.*

Matt removes all the visible fat from the bird he's going to use in the pot, and when he's cutting up the other bird he removes all fat and most of the skin. He throws all this in a skillet and cooks slowly over medium heat, pouring off fat as it accumulates. He saves the fat for the various uses mentioned throughout this book.

The small pieces of meat and skin eventually become crisp. This is dog candy. We store it in the refrigerator and use it as doggie treats for Bucky.

That's all there is to it.

Molasses Doggie "Doughnuts"

These have a soft, chewy, almost cakey texture perfect for elderly dogs. If you want a hard, crunchy texture, reduce the amount of baking powder and bake at a lower temperature for a longer time. They're not as sweet as the amount of molasses might suggest; try one yourself and you'll see.

2 eggs
2 tablespoons rendered chicken fat, softened at
   room temperature
¼ cup molasses
2 cups unbleached all-purpose flour
2 teaspoons baking powder

Beat eggs until fluffy. Beat in chicken fat, then beat in molasses a little at a time. Mix well.

Sift flour with baking powder. Add to wet mixture and stir thoroughly.

Turn out dough onto lightly floured board and knead until all flour is incorporated and dough is silky, about 3 minutes. Roll out with rolling pin to a uniform ¼-inch thickness. Cut out pieces with a doughnut cutter or cookie cutter.

Place doughnuts and holes in well-seasoned cast iron #8 skillet or on a lightly greased cookie sheet. For a soft, chewy texture, bake in preheated 350-degree oven for 20 minutes, or until a toothpick comes out clean. Remove skillet from oven; remove doughnuts and holes to a rack to cool.

Makes 10 doughnuts and holes, enough to just fill the #8 skillet.

Chicken Biscklets

These are light, crumbly, and so flavorful you might want to eat them youself. Sorry, doggie.

1 cup unbleached all-purpose flour
1 teaspoon salt
2 teaspoons baking powder
½ cup chicken fat, rendered and allowed to harden
4 tablespoons evaporated milk

Sift dry ingredients together. Cut in chicken fat. Add evaporated milk and stir thoroughly. (If you have leftover milk mixture from having made **Pan de Tres Leches,** you can use it here.)

Turn out onto lightly floured board. Knead dough gently and briefly, just until it holds together well.

Roll out with a rolling pin to a uniform height of about a half inch. To cut out the biscklets, you'll need something smaller in diameter than the traditional biscuit cutter. A liqueur glass is perfect, if you have such a thing.

Place biscklets in an ungreased #8 cast iron skillet, or if you've come this far in this book and still don't own a cast iron skillet, use a cookie sheet.

Bake in preheated 450 degree oven 25–30 minutes, or less. Keep an eye on them and remove from oven when they're golden brown. Remove from skillet and place on cooling rack until you can't stand it any longer and have to taste one, but be careful: they retain heat.

Makes about a dozen biscklets of 2" in diameter.

Pictured facing page, middle of picture, below Molasses Doggie "Doughnuts."

Charcoal Chews

It's said that charcoal biscuits are good for your dog's teeth, breath, and digestion, and that may be. But all he cares about is that it taste good. That's another reason to use bacon fat instead of Crisco.

If you burn a wood stove, you have access to charcoal. Take out some clean chunks before you throw away the detritus from last night's fire. Grind them in a mortar with a pestle, the old-fashioned way. If you're worried about breathing any resultant charcoal dust, just tie a wet bandanna around your face, as the cowboys did.

½ cup whole wheat flour
1 cup unbleached all-purpose flour
¾ cup ground charcoal
6 tablespoons solidified rendered bacon fat,
  or Crisco as a last resort
12 tablespoons ice water

Mix together the flours and the ground charcoal. Cut in solidified bacon fat till you have pea-sized pieces. Gradually add ice water and stir with a fork until blended.

Turn out onto a piece of waxed paper. Form into a ball. Roll lightly with a rolling pin, trying for a uniform thickness of about ¼ inch.

Use a biscuit cutter to cut out circles of dough, then slice each circle into quarters. Place these little pie-shaped pieces—and the bone-shaped pieces between circles—into an ungreased cast iron skillet. You'll most likely need a #8, with a #5 for the overflow.

Bake in preheated 450-degree oven for 15 minutes, then turn heat down to 300 degrees and bake an additional 45 minutes. Makes about three dozen.

I didn't taste these myself, but Bucky sure gave his stamp of approval.

Pictured page 158, bottom of picture, below Chicken Biscklets.

Food Items

beef "bullets"
If you haven't the time or inclination to make your own concentrated stocks, you can purchase them (at a price) from
www.morethangourmet.com

blue agave nectar
If your local supermarket doesn't carry this in its baking section, try
www.blueagavenectar.com

Bragg's liquid amino seasoning
Available in health food sections of supermarkets.

dried wild mushrooms
www.pistolrivermushrooms.com
excellent selection, excellent service

guajillo chiles
If you can't find these in the Mexican foods section of your local supermarket, try
www.gourmetsleuth.com

hoisin sauce
Look for this in the Asiatic foods section of your local supermarket, or available online at
www.mingspantry.com

kombu
www.diamondorganics.com

Larrupin' mustard-dill sauce
www.larrupingoods.com

Marigold bouillon powder
www.aroracreations.com

Mexican chocolate
www.mexgrocer.com

natural black walnut flavor
> The Spicery Shoppe, Downers Grove, IL 60515
> www.flavorchem.com/spiceryshoppe/nonalc.htm
> or Butte Creek Mill, Eagle Point, Oregon
> www.buttecreekmill.com
> or www.barryfarm.com

nopalitos
> Product and recipes available online at
> www.mexgrocer.com

reduction sauces
> www.morethangourmet.com

Sap Sago cheese
> www.igourmet.com
> We order these a dozen at a time, to make the shipping
> costs go further. They keep practically forever.

Thai peanut satay sauce
> Try the Asiatic foods section of your local
> supermarket, or if they don't carry it, order from
> www.templeofthai.com

Equipment

chinois
> There's a nice stainless steel one at
> www.cooking.com

electronic kitchen scale
> Salter makes one for about $40. Find it online at
> www.metrokitchen.com

electronic kitchen timer
> Ours is by Westbend, but there as many different
> styles of timer as there are shapes of teapots. Browse
> a bunch at www.kitchen-upgrades.com

instant-read thermometer
> Readily available, but if you can't find one locally, try
> www.comforthouse.com/foodthermom.html

large coarse strainer
> You can find this and any other strainer—or, for that
> matter, just about any quality kitchen accessory—at
> www.williams-sonoma.com

mandoline
For a quality mandoline, one good online source is www.williams-sonoma.com

parchment paper
If you can't find it in your local supermarket, try www.kingarthurflour.com/shop

remote thermometer with meat probe
Polder makes a good one. If you can't find it at your local hardware store, try www.cooking.com

stockpots with spigots
These can be difficult to find. Ours are big, heavy, and expensive . . . but worth it. Made by Matfer Bourgeat, they were located for us by Alyson's Kitchen, of Ashland, Oregon. Alyson's Kitchen can order them for you, or you can order direct from www.culinarycookware.com

ulu
Where else?
www.ulu.com

vacuum sealer
Don't be seduced by a cheapie. Buy the best in the beginning and save yourself a lot of frustration. www.cabelas.com

Advice and Support

For specific tips, instructions, and a pictorial of how to clean and season your pans, visit the Wagner and Griswold Society website at www.wag-society.org. These friendly members have a forum where you can ask questions and identify your cast iron cookware for free. You might even consider becoming a member of this group to receive their newsletter and participate in their annual conventions.

Glossary

beef bullets

Matt's term for an intensely concentrated stock.

chinois

A cone-shaped sieve with a closely woven mesh for straining sauces. Also known as "China hat."

deglaze

To dilute and scrape meat sediments left in pan after browning meat in order to make a sauce, typically using wine.

fond

Sediments left on the bottom of a pan after browning or sautéing meat.

mirepoix

A mixture of sautéed chopped vegetables used in making a sauce for meat or fish. Frequently the mirepoix is discarded and the sauce is strained after the flavors have been extracted from the vegetables.

mise en place

Frequently used items kept at the cooking station.

parboil

To partially cook food by boiling. Parboiling salt pork before rendering can help leach out the extra salt.

side rag

A square of terry-cloth toweling used to handle hot pans or pots in place of a hot mitt.

try out

Render, melt down fats.

ulu

Eskimo woman's knife resembling a food chopper with a crescent-shaped blade.

About Us

The meals we produce together, our lives as a married couple . . . this book . . . are all collaborations. Whether salubriating at our cabin in the woods or pursuing our careers from our home in the city, we complement each other in many ways.

Throughout this book we use the first-person voice, though as you may surmise, the speaker may be either of us—the differences are usually apparent, but we leave you to guess who is saying what. (A hint: When we first came together as a couple, he said, "Well, here's the deal. I really, really like to cook, so if you don't mind, I'll do the dinners . . . you can do the salads and desserts, if you'd like?" And that's the way it's been ever since. Except for Monday night football.)

All of Matt's recipes he has dictated as he paces. Linda has done her best to stifle the English teacher in her and allow Matt's often wacky and slightly irreverent vernacular to shine through, in the belief that you, dear reader, will enjoy it as much as she does.

No book is without error, typographical or otherwise. Any book can be improved with input from readers. So please send us your questions, comments, suggestions, and corrections (see copyright page and take your pick of e-mail addresses). Be assured that we *will* reply.

31901046549020